THE ORIGINS OF
CHRISTIAN PHILOSOPHY

By CLAUDE TRESMONTANT

Translated from the French by MARK PONTIFEX, O.S.B.

HAWTHORN BOOKS · PUBLISHERS · *New York*

First Edition, January, 1963

NIHIL OBSTAT

Daniel Duivesteijn, S.T.D.

 Censor Deputatus

IMPRIMATUR

E. Morrogh Bernard

 Vicarius Generalis

Westmonasterii, die XXII OCTOBRIS MCMLXII

2 - 11 - 63 *mar* 163

H-9529

CONTENTS

INTRODUCTION

Philosophy is simply the examination by the human understanding, starting from the data of reality, of a number of
problems not found on the level of scientific, experimental
research, but yet concerned with the rational order. When
the structure of the atom or the economy of the living cell
or the laws which determine the process of biological evolution or those which govern statistical systems, and so on,
are analysed—and this can only be done incompletely—
there still remains a set of problems which have not yet
been dealt with, and which human reason wishes to investi-
gate. For instance, when we consider the fact of cosmic and
biological evolution, the question remains whether this cosmic
evolutionary process occurs as the result of a purely immanent
power, in other words, whether the cosmic process is self-
creative, whether it is the absolute, or on the other hand
whether it implies a reference, to make it intelligible, to a
cause which is both immanent and transcendent as its explanation. Is this synthesis, which takes place throughout the
cosmic evolution, the work of elements in combination? Does
the composition of complex matter come from more simple
particles? Is multiplicity sufficient to account for the organ-
isms in which it occurs and receives a form? Or, on the contrary, are we to say that every synthesis transcends the elements
of which it is composed? When we consider reality, whether
cosmic, physical, biological, psychological or human, questions of this kind inevitably arise. They are not questions
within the sphere of positive experimental science, but within
a sphere of their own. This rational sphere, distinct from that
of the positive sciences, is the sphere of philosophy.

We all know that, especially in the last century, some thinkers have tended to neglect the existence, the legitimacy, the necessity, of this special philosophical order. They claim that science is enough, that it alone covers the whole rational field: it is this tendency which has been called positivism. But such an attitude breaks down, both in the scientific sphere, and in the broadly rational sphere, as the result of an overwhelming internal pressure. For whatever man does, and in whatever way he does it, he can never get away from philosophy. Even though he does not wish it, as has been said long ago, he must still be a philosopher.

Marxism, to take an example, is not a scientific positivism.[1] Marxism is a philosophy which claims to rest on positive sciences alone, but yet it makes assertions which are, strictly speaking, metaphysical, wholly transcending—make no mistake about it—the assertions of positive science. Marxism teaches formally and dogmatically that the world is uncreated, self-created, eternal, infinite in time and space: this is to take up a metaphysical position. Indeed no one can fail to take up a metaphysical position, whether explicitly or implicitly. You have only to look closely at a rationalist and positivist thinker. Search in all the nooks and corners of his thought. You will find that latent philosophical assumptions soon appear, which live hidden there with their own life, and have scarcely ever been questioned or critically examined, never swept up, so to speak, by the brush of criticism. One rationalist scientist will show himself at heart a pantheist, perhaps with a special attraction to Indian mysticism; another will be led to follow Spinoza, or, unconsciously, Plotinus. We can no more get away from metaphysics than from living in a universe governed by such laws as gravitation. Thought has inevitably a metaphysical structure because the universe,

---

[1] At the present day, and in the case of some Marxists, it is sometimes reduced to this.

which is subject to physical laws, has also a metaphysical structure.

So long as they have existed, human beings have always philosophized. It is possible to philosophize either explicitly, as did Plato, Aristotle and Descartes, or implicitly. In the Egyptian and Assyro-Babylonian mythologies, in the myths which abound among the religions of India, Oceania, Africa or Greece, metaphysical assertions are implicitly made. Thus, when the cosmogonic Egyptian and Assyro-Babylonian mythologies (adopted by Hesiod) suppose as the principle of all things a watery chaos from which come the gods, the world and man, this amounts to saying, if put explicitly, that in these religions the chaos is the absolute, and the gods are not. The theogenic and cosmogenic processes are carried on parallel to one another. There is a coming into being of the divine element as there is of the world. The divine element is not, strictly speaking, the absolute. The first principle, the uncreated, the eternal, the source of all, is the primitive chaos. This involves conclusions in the sphere of philosophy.

These religions also teach that man was made from the spittle, the blood or the seed of a god, and this too involves metaphysical teaching. It means, in abstract terms, that according to these religions man was made from the god's substance, that he is consubstantial with the god—an idea which reappears in the Gnostic and Manichaean systems.

Systems of thought, even mythological and religious, thus imply a metaphysical structure, and metaphysical beliefs, at least implicitly, which we have to draw out and bring to light.

If we analyse the material which is offered us by the history of religion at the present day, we find that all religions possess a metaphysical content in themselves. And we see, too, that the philosophies strictly so-called—what we are accustomed in modern times to call "philosophy"—are much more dependent than has hitherto been realized on metaphysical beliefs implicitly contained in the religions out of which these philosophies have in fact emerged. Thus the Platonism of the *Phaedo*, the *Phaedrus* or the *Republic* owes much to the mystery religions: this had already been recognized. But the mystery religions owe much to ancient mythologies whose roots run back into the remotest past, and it is thus clear that the Platonic teaching about the soul as a part of the divine, which has fallen into an evil body in which it is exiled away from its home, is a philosophic survival of a primitive mythological theme, certainly expressed in Orphism, but also before that in Brahmanism. Our own teaching about the "soul" and the "body", even at the present day, coming through Plato and Descartes, is derived from Orphism. We are a long way from pure rationalism!

The religious tradition of the Bible, both Jewish and Christian, like other religious traditions, also possesses a religious content or structure, that is to say, beliefs which, whether explicitly or implicitly, are truly metaphysical. I shall examine this content later on. But, apart from that, what we must notice is that the metaphysical content of the religious tradition of the Bible, both Jewish and Christian, is utterly different from the metaphysical content or structure of the religious traditions of India, Africa, Oceania or Greece. All religious traditions have a metaphysical structure, but they are not all the same. The character of Hebrew religion, Jewish and Christian, is such as to involve a metaphysical structure which is original and exceptional.

Now we can already see on the horizon the problem which will confront us. If the philosophic systems, such as Platonism, Aristotelianism, Stoicism or Neoplatonism, are in fact derived from metaphysical structures or metaphysical principles contained in religious traditions and religious tendencies, what happens when these philosophic systems meet a system of thought derived from a religious tradition whose metaphysical principles are utterly different, the Hebrew tradition, Jewish and Christian?

We must of course choose our language carefully. The mythological influence, or mythological heritage, is less in the case of Aristotle than in that of Plato or Plotinus. Aristotle in his youth was deeply influenced by Orphic beliefs; as he developed, his attitude changed. Instead of starting with Orphic myths, he attempted to establish a philosophy on the basis of concrete experience. His philosophy is thus more *rational* than that of his master Plato, and of his distant follower Plotinus. We shall see the result of this in connection with Christian thought.

Mention of Aristotle, in connection with the religious traditions of his time and of his environment, takes us at once to the great problem which will occupy us throughout this book. I have said that Aristotle, for instance on the problem of the soul, was freed from traces of Orphism, and dealt with the problem of the soul in a far more positive fashion, approaching it from a new angle. Instead of repeating the Orphic idea of the divine soul fallen into an evil body, where it would have lost the memory of its divine essence, Aristotle starts from experience. He finds out that in the concrete individual, which is bodily, the form and the unified many constitute a single being. If the form is removed, there is no longer a body but the many of matter. If the many, if matter, is removed, nothing remains. A dead finger is only a finger by homonymy, like a finger in a picture. The concrete individual is composed of matter and form, but the union of these two is not a "fall". The union of soul and matter, which it informs, is not a "descent" of a pre-existing soul into a "body", imagined like a vessel. The body does not exist before the soul exists.

When he goes on to a rational and empirical analysis Aristotle proceeds as a philosopher. He puts aside Orphic myths handed down by his master Plato, and to be repeated by Plotinus. What he did was to philosophize.

But, if so, can we speak of Christian philosophy?

Philosophy is a rational exercise of free thought based on experience. The practice of philosophy is an activity essentially distinct from the *passivity* which seems to characterize religious belief. Between the act of reasoning, of reflecting on the real, and the assent of belief to a myth or a dogma, what connection can there be? What is there common to reason and faith? I am purposely putting the problem in its most acute form.

All the religious traditions, those of India, Egypt, Babylonia, Phoenicia, Greece, as of Judea, involve a metaphysical structure. True though this is, the metaphysical structure is not yet, strictly speaking, philosophy, since, as I have said, many of these metaphysical implications involved in ancient religions are, or appear to be, purely mythological. Does not the exercise of philosophy consist in getting free from the metaphysical implications involved in these religions, in order to discover the true metaphysical structure of the real? Undoubtedly it does.

The Hebrew religious tradition, Jewish and Christian, carries with it a metaphysical structure which is original, specific and unique of its kind. That is what will appear in the course of this book. But is not this metaphysical structure involved in the tradition of biblical thought just as mythological as the metaphysical structure involved in Brahmanism, Orphism or totem religions? We must examine this question, and we shall perhaps be greatly surprised when we find that the metaphysical structure of biblical theology is not mythological but is on the contrary *positive*, paying due regard to the real as we experience it, suited to the real, open to the real. If the metaphysical structure of biblical theology were mythological, like Brahmanism or Orphism, the relation between "Christian philosophy" and biblical theology would be analogous to, or of the same order as, the relation which exists between the philosophies of Plato, of Plotinus (or of Schelling and Hegel), and the ancient Hellenic religious traditions. We should not have, strictly speaking, a Christian *philosophy*, because we should not have a free and independent exercise of pure reason based on experience. We should only have a commentary on, or conceptual formulation of, metaphysical data, still quite penetrated with mythology. It should be plainly said: the philosophies of Plato, of Plotinus, like those of Spinoza, of Fichte, of Hegel, of Schelling, and finally of Marx, are far from being freed from the mythological content they inherited through ancient Greek philosophy and ancient Hellenic religions. The myths of the divinity of the soul, of the soul's pre-existence, of the soul's fall, the deification of the stars, the myth of the everlasting return, the theogonic myths which influence the religious philosophy of Hegel, the metaphysical theories which give the world the attributes of the absolute, aseity, infinity, eternity, ontological independence and so on, and which amount to deifying the cosmos, just as Heraclitus and Aristotle did, all this pre-rational, and indeed irrational, material haunts philosophy to the present day. Our freethinkers are less free than they suppose, and are still very religious, though devotees of religions which flourished many centuries before our era. Modern philosophy in fact still owes much to Egyptian, Assyro-Babylonian, Greek, and even Indian, religions, which flourished before Christianity.

But does not Christianity itself, and with it "Christian philosophy", owe much to Hebrew mythologies which we find expressed in the first chapter of Genesis? We shall see what is the answer the more deeply we meditate on this problem of Christian philosophy, the closer we approach, in concentric and centripetal circles, the ultimate problem—that of truth.

Let us set down our meditations. If philosophy is the free and autonomous use of the human understanding based on experience alone, there is no more a "Christian" philosophy than Christian mathematics or Christian physics. Before

Bréhier, Blondel had already said this in his *Lettre* of 1896. If, then, philosophy is what I have said—and I think it is— there is no more a Christian philosophy than Christian mathematics. Philosophy is the same for all, since it is the exercise of pure reason common to all. Nevertheless this must be added: neither is there Greek philosophy, or German philosophy, or French philosophy, any more than there is Greek, German or French, mathematics. Philosophy is no more national than mathematics.

There is no more a philosophy of Plato, Spinoza, Descartes, Kant or Marx than a mathematics peculiar to them. Philosophy, like mathematics, belongs to no individual; it is common to all. Yet we speak of the geometry of Euclid or Riemann, of the mechanics of Newton or Einstein. All books on philosophy deal with the philosophies of Plato, Aristotle, the Stoics and so on. Histories of philosophy contain chapters or volumes devoted to "Greek philosophy", "French philosophy" or "German philosophy".

Strictly speaking, then, there is no more a Christian philosophy than a German, English or Turkish philosophy; or than there is Chinese mathematics or Russian mathematics, or than there is a conservative science or a progressive science. There is no more a socialist than a conservative and reactionary astronomy or genetics. Science and reason are the same for all.

In fact, however, there exist systems of philosophy, Greek, German, English and so on; of Plato, Aristotle, Plotinus, St Thomas, Descartes, Kant, Marx and so on. There even exist systems of geometry or mechanics.

The further we explore the subject the more our difficulties increase, and our problems become more complex.

Christianity itself professes to provide the world with a metaphysic which is of universal value, because it is *true*. Christianity, so far as it is concerned, is ready to renounce the epithet, Christian, as applied to philosophy. It asks nothing more than that its philosophy should be called simply philosophy, since, in its eyes, it is in fact the one true philosophy.

Non-Christian philosophers, however, do not agree. Neoplatonist philosophers, whether Celsus, Porphyry, Spinoza or Bréhier, think that Christian metaphysics rest on metaphysical principles which are fundamentally false. The idea of creation, wrote Fichte, is the ultimate error in philosophy. Thus non-Christian philosophers describe as "Christian" that "philosophy" which developed from the rise of Christianity in the society formed by the Church. They call their own philosophy philosophy in the true sense, their own metaphysics rational, which is that of Plato, Plotinus, Porphyry or Spinoza, teaching the divine and eternal character of the world, the everlasting cycle, the essential divinity of the soul. Christians, on their side, regard these views as irrational and mythological.

Disagreement about the nature of philosophy is due to disagreement about the nature of truth.

There will only be one philosophy when all men are agreed about truth. Meanwhile there are many philosophies. There is a Platonic, Aristotelian, Kantian, Marxist philosophy and so on, and there is also a Christian philosophy, which has its own structure, principles and theories forming an harmonious and original system.

Christian philosophy is not the same as that of Plato, Plotinus, Spinoza, Hegel or Marx. The metaphysical outlook and principles, the tendencies natural to it, are radically and fundamentally different—we may go so far as to say utterly opposed.

But the field has not yet been completely cleared in preparation for what will be said. Perhaps at the end of these few pages the reader will agree that there exists a metaphysical structure, original and peculiar to Christianity, but he will not necessarily be convinced that this metaphysical structure is *philosophical*, that is, the work of reason.

I have already pointed out that at the centre of the forest we are entering there will be found not a wild beast but the problem of truth. That, however, is not all. In this forest there are noxious plants and weeds: misunderstandings implicit and unrecognized, false assumptions. One of these false assumptions is concerned with the inspiration of the Bible. You may ask what this has to do with our present problem. We shall soon see.

The problem may be put like this. Christians have received, in a wholly passive way, the deposit of Scripture which they regard as holy and inspired. Scripture, or rather the Scriptures (those "wild Oriental writings", as Maurras called them), have been declared to Jewish prophets. Let us agree that these Scriptures contain, at least implicitly, metaphysical teaching. Christians employ this biblical metaphysic, and impose it on their Church. None of this is philosophy, for philosophy is a free act of the mind, an independent intellectual activity, recognizing no external authority other than reality as experienced. Christians are quite right to retain and continue "biblical metaphysics", but all the same they are not forming a philosophy. They are perpetuating a mythology, just like those philosophers who are still indebted to Orphism or Brahmanism, which led the German philosophers so far astray in the Romantic period.

We reply: this objection rests on a false idea of inspiration, and, more generally, on the economy and law of understanding within faith; your objection also rests on a false idea of faith. In order to grasp this notion of Christian philosophy, at least a few words must be said about this fresh difficulty.

In the Old Testament inspiration is not the same as dictation received quite passively by the inspired author. This idea of inspiration is anthropomorphic. The supernatural inspiration of Scripture does not mean that the prophet is reduced to the state of a lifeless instrument. This would be unworthy both of him and of the Holy Ghost who inspires him. Inspiration is not a forcible intrusion from outside, a sheer conquest by the Spirit of God of a human being who is reduced to the state of a mere thing (rather like a conquest from the air such as occurs in modern warfare). Inspiration is not to be looked at as an act of violence; the Fathers tell us that God does not do acts of violence. To attribute violence to God and to his ways of acting is to attribute a human character to him, to fall into anthropomorphism. God's power is gentle. Inspiration does not mean that the human spirit is "occupied" by God, invaded by him and dominated, so that conquered humanity is wiped out. Quite the contrary: supernatural inspiration is always from the very first a redemption, that is, a liberation and regeneration, regeneration of human reason and human freedom, which have been cast down, enfeebled and left prostrate under the weight of sin, that blinds the eyes of the understanding, freedom from the service of idols which are the work of man's hands and thought. In fact supernatural inspiration, as it acts in the Old Testament, has brought about the most powerful movement and renewal of thought that has ever occurred. All peoples, all civilizations, worshipped the sun, the moon, the stars, deified emperors, even beasts (totems), and natural forces (reproductive and so on). The Hebrews were the only people who did not worship sun, moon, stars, men, beasts, natural forces, wood, stone or iron, and who refused to sacrifice living children to lifeless idols.

Here we have an intellectual revolution, a liberation, an act of free thought, a rejection of myth, an effort to use reason, undoubtedly the most important that the human race has known in all its history. On the day when Abraham left Ur of the Chaldees, when he ceased to worship the moon and stars, to sacrifice to the idols of his fathers, and when he started for a country which he knew not, called by a God who is not identified with any visible thing, he brought about the greatest, and at the same time the most hidden, of revolutions (life is conceived during the night), the most decisive for the human race.

When the prophets of Israel bitterly rebuke pagan idolatry, they are doing something strictly *rational*. When they refuse to sacrifice human children to idols or to myths, they carry their work of the use of reason into practical human conduct. Contemporary paganism has still much to learn from them in this matter, as in others.

The inspiration which has led to this intellectual revolution, this renewal of mankind, is not something "dictated" and imposed from without on a servile human instrument. It is a liberation which works from within, and which starts to create a new, holy, reasonable humanity, renouncing the worship of the stars, the forces of vegetation, kings and beasts, and the sacrifice of human children to bloodstained idols. The rebirth of reason is accompanied by the rebirth of the whole man. Lastly, understanding does not grow without holiness. The whole problem of Christian philosophy is to be seen in this fact: understanding can go astray by and through sin, wickedness, idolatry, concupiscence, vanity, passion and falsehood. To free the understanding and render it capable of truth the whole man must be set free. The understanding is not an isolated power. There is no knowledge of the truth without justice. True philosophy, we are told by Blondel, is the holiness of reason.

Inspiration, then, does not use man as a merely passive instrument. Supernatural inspiration frees and regenerates man, stirs his understanding, expands it and carries it to the full development of its power and capacity. From a purely human point of view men like Jeremias, Isaias or the nameless prophet whose sayings have been joined with those of Isaias, form types of humanity outstanding for their understanding, power, holiness and the richness of their minds. These are not "instruments" or "things", mere pens in God's hand. They are fellow workmen with God, roused up, created, by him. Hence there exists in the very centre of biblical theology, in the very centre of all biblical tradition, a rational *human* activity which cooperates with the grace of inspiration. In relation to the ancient religions the prophets of Israel are freethinkers and rationalists. At the heart of that development which constitutes biblical theology there is an exercise of human reason. The idea of inspiration which is too often held is a *Monophysite* idea, which misrepresents the human share, the part taken by human nature, in the Bible. The Bible is not a book which has fallen from heaven (the image of an attack from the air is always returning). The Bible is a book born amid mankind but coming from God, in the manner of an Incarnation, whereby nature is not destroyed but healed and raised to a higher state to reach its perfection.

So this metaphysical structure in biblical thought, which I shall briefly explain later on, is not imposed on mankind from outside; it is not received passively by man. It is the fruit of regenerated, free, newly created, human understanding.

The other mistake which confronts us as we enter on this question, and which entangles us when we try to penetrate the vast country we have to survey, is an analogous error, and concerns faith.

Christians believe too often at the present day, and consequently non-Christians with them, that Christian faith is a belief resulting from a choice, an arbitrary decision, an act of the will, known as "an act of faith".

Now faith, according to the orthodox Christian view, is not what Plato calls opinion, the last and lowest form of thought. Faith, in the orthodox Christian view, is a free, supernatural, understanding, informed by the Holy Ghost, a genuine knowledge, a judgement, the supreme form and highest activity of thought. Faith is a free act because understanding itself is a free act, because understanding can be lost by and through sin, as I have already pointed out. But faith is also a rational act, with a reasonable basis and a content which we can understand, though informed supernaturally by grace and by the Spirit.

When Christians receive the scriptural deposit they do not on that account cease to be human beings and to think. On the contrary, just as with inspiration, Christian faith stirs and wakens understanding, frees it and raises it up. Human understanding is at work within the activity of Christian theology, in cooperation with the grace of God. There exists within the tradition of Christian thought a genuine use of reason, fully rational, fully independent (this does not mean separated), and distinct from that movement by which we receive a truth which comes from God.

There is a Christian *philosophy*, because human reason operates actually within Christian theology, with full freedom, without constraint or enfeeblement, but on the contrary ever freely, gladly and vigorously, through the very movement of revelation.

We can see how the idea of cooperation proves to be fundamental. There is a Christian philosophy because there is cooperation of human freedom with God's grace, of human freedom with the work of theology, cooperation between human thought and the word of God. Theologies which deny the possibility of such cooperation (theologies which sprang from the Reformation) must also deny the possibility of a natural theology, of the natural knowledge of God and of a Christian philosophy.

CONCLUSIONS OF THE INTRODUCTION

There exists—I shall make this claim once again—a metaphysical structure, original, inherent in Christian theology as in biblical theology. There exists a Christian metaphysic.

There exists, too, at the heart of traditional Christian thought, a free and independent activity of human reason, based on experience, ready to receive the word of God. There exists a Christian *philosophy*, because human reason, within the Christian society, is not reduced to the condition of a passive instrument, to the condition of a slave. On the contrary, redemption affects reason and understanding, no less than freedom and conduct.

We shall see confirmation of both these assertions in the pages that follow.

THE SOURCES OF CHRISTIAN METAPHYSICS IN THE BIBLE

Christian metaphysics have their sources in the tradition, in the setting, of biblical thought. We must go further and say: Christian metaphysics carry on the metaphysics contained in biblical theology. Biblical metaphysics and Christian metaphysics in outline are the same. It is the same metaphysical system that develops, from the great theologian whom biblical criticism has called the Jahvist right up to the Vatican Council.

Christian metaphysics are organically united to Christian theology. Or better, Christian theology possesses a certain metaphysical structure peculiar to itself. To deal with certain metaphysical principles is to deal also—and sometimes with danger to oneself—with certain essential principles of Christian theology. This point will appear again more than once. Only a particular kind of theology is compatible with a particular kind of metaphysics. We shall have to return to this point too.

Now, orthodox Christian theology is based on biblical theology, on the Old and the New Testament. The New Testament does not contradict the Old Testament, but continues and completes it. From Genesis to the Apocalypse it is the same manifestation of God which is progressively at work. Throughout the whole history of God's people the same God manifests himself. In the person of Jesus of Nazareth the God of Abraham is manifested in person, without created intermediary. Christianity does not contradict the Judaism of the Law and the Prophets; it perfects it, as the fruit is the perfection of the tree, as adult age is the perfection of childhood. Orthodox Christian theology regards all Scripture, Old and New Testaments, as God's word; it is based on Scripture.

We can thus understand why the metaphysical principles, the metaphysical requirements, involved in Christian theology and constitutive of Christian theology, are found already manifested in biblical theology. Hence it is in its biblical source that we must look for the first origins of Christian philosophy, or, in other words, its prehistory.

Israel, as I said in the Introduction, brought about in the world a revolution the scope of which we tend to minimize at the present day. The peoples adored the sun, moon, stars and natural forces, and worshipped stones, wood, iron, deified kings and totems. Alone among mankind Israel rejected this cosmic animism, this making sacred the sensible world, this turning sensible objects into gods. Israel lay at the source of modern rationalism so far as it is an advance. This revolution has been decisive, radical, almost violent. It was an uprooting, a new birth: "Go forth out of thy country, and from thy kindred, and out of thy father's house, and come into the land which I shall show thee. And I will make of thee a great nation" (Gen. 12. 1–2). When he left his family and his country Abraham also left the worship of the moon, the religion of his fathers, to follow an Unknown, which had neither image nor statue in its temples. Instead of worshipping the visible moon, the visible statues of Moloch or Baal, the visible King, Israel worshipped an invisible being who was not of this world. Nothing belonging to this world is divine or worthy of worship.

This "atheism", as it seemed in comparison with the many gods of the pagan peoples, this uprooting from worship of gods perceptible to the senses, this change of attitude, of thought and of heart, which turned them away from gods of nature, and led them to him who has no visible form, the hidden God—this was a revolution in the metaphysical, ethical, theological and even the political order. Instead of worshipping a king, as did the Babylonians and Egyptians, instead of making a human king into a god, Israel now knew that the Living God was the King of Israel, and the prophets of old opposed the idea that Israel should take a human king like other nations, for then the people might easily practise a "cult of personality", as we say at the present day of the rulers and dictators of modern states.

The absolute, the divine, sought for by pagan nations then and still at the present day in objects around them, in the universe, in visible beings, Israel knew must be sought elsewhere and in other ways. Plato, Aristotle and Plotinus regarded the world as divine. Israel, alone among the nations, dared to say that the world is not divine, not uncreated, not eternal. Free thought has never been so bold, so blasphemous in relation to the ideas of the holy then commonly held.

The world is not the absolute, nor is anything which the world contains. Even at the present day metaphysical systems (often without recognizing it), like that of Marx, attribute once again to the universe the attributes of the absolute, aseity, eternity, ontological self-sufficiency, just as did Heraclitus or Aristotle. To regard the universe as sacred is not, therefore, a tendency of ancient times alone, characteristic only of ancient religions and philosophies. It is also a tendency of the present day, and we find it expressed in the main stream of modern pantheistic philosophy from the time of Spinoza.

When Israel discovered that the world was not the absolute and was not the divine, it discovered too (though the process worked rather in the other direction) that the divine was other than the world. Or rather, by discovering the living God, Israel discovered that he was not the world, and that the world was not divine.

This fundamental distinction between the absolute and the world may be called the fundamental discovery, in the field of metaphysics, of biblical theology.

The absolute is distinct from the world. But what, then, is the relation between the absolute and the world? A relation that the Bible alone has known, and which it expresses by a term reserved for God, of which the subject in the Hebrew text is always God: *bara*, to create.

There are of course in the ancient religions and philosophies theogonic and cosmogonic myths, stories of the generation and formation of the world. In the *Timaeus* of Plato there is a demiurge. But nowhere is there found a doctrine of creation in the strict and technical meaning of the word.

The doctrine of creation in biblical thought implies that God made the world and all that it contains without using any pre-existing matter, without starting from a pre-existing chaos, a pre-existing disorder which he had to set in order, and without drawing from his own substance the beings he created. Creation is not in the human sense a fashioning of something, nor is it generation.

To fashion a thing is not to create it for the very reason that the matter itself is not fashioned, but is present from the beginning. The human workman takes some material, wood, stone or iron, and makes a table, a boat, a house or a sword. He does not create the material. According to biblical theology —and in this it differs from all ancient cosmogonic myths— God creates matter, he creates everything, he does not use anything which already exists, he needs nothing, he looks for no previous material. Generation of gods from one another, the fashioning of men from the divine substance (blood, spittle, seed) is not creation. In the Egyptian and Assyro-Babylonian cosmogonies man is made from the substance of the god. This substance is itself uncreated, but is, so to speak, the material of which man is made. Here there is no real creation of a new being in no way pre-existent; the divine substance of which it is made already exists.

At the present day when a young writer gives us a description of his own life in his first novel (an only too frequent temptation), he does not create a character; he gives us his flesh and blood, he confides himself to us, he makes a confession of his life or boasts of it, he opens his heart to us. The novelist who *creates* a character (which is very rarely done) is he who can invent a being who is not made of his own substance but fundamentally different from himself, who has an existence, a character, a nature, other than that of the author. We are not parts of the divine substance, but creatures of God. A decisive metaphysical revolution has taken place, and has not ceased to bear fruit, far from it.

The biblical idea of creation is the keystone of biblical theology and of biblical metaphysics, of Christian theology and metaphysics. According to Scripture, according to Judaism, Christianity and Islam, the absolute is not the world. The absolute is creator of the world. The relation which exists between the absolute and the world is a relation of creation.

This doctrine of creation is taught from the very beginning of the Bible, and is no chance event. The theological school which biblical critics refer to by the sign P (fifth century: *Priestercodex*), and which has produced that liturgical recital which comes at the beginning of the Bible, has rightly set the first stone at the foundation of Scripture, as it is at the foundation of the world, "In the beginning God created heaven and earth."...

The absolute is creator of heaven and earth. This means that we are radically distinct from the absolute, and hence can have the relations with it of one person with another, as would not be possible were we only an emanation from it or a part of its substance.

What is the reason for creation? The priestly recital at the beginning of the Bible does not tell us, but it does tell us much simply by recounting the fact of creation and the order in which it occurred.

This account makes no mention of, and indeed goes out of its way to reject, all theogonic mythology. At the beginning was God. There is no genealogy of gods, no genesis of the divine, as in the Egyptian, Babylonian, Orphic mythologies, or in the poems of Hesiod, or in the later Gnostic speculations, or finally in the philosophy of Hegel. God is at the beginning, not chaos. There is no war between the gods, no theomachy, no destruction or separation, no *Entzweiung* or *Entfremdung*, as in theosophical speculations. God is free and sovereign in his creative act. God has no *need* to create in order to realize himself, to beget children, or to become aware of himself. There is no theosophy in this basic account.

Later, or at least further on, in the Bible we are told who God is, and can see how God loves creation which is his work, how he loves mankind whom he has created, that new people he raises up and who are meant to be the source of a new human race: the Wisdom of God takes pleasure in playing amid the children of men. The whole Old Testament is a romance of love, between God and the Virgin of Israel, Jerusalem, the first fruits of the new and holy humanity. The key to Holy Scripture is to be found in the Song of Songs; the reason for creation is a union, a love match. This is how, much later, both Jewish and Christian mystics have understood it. The New Testament repeats this analogy of marriage, not only the Gospels but also St Paul and the Apocalypse. A letter of St John gives us the very definition of the absolute: God is *agape*. I do not venture to translate this word, which in our language can only be given a corresponding term that lowers its meaning, is ambiguous, suggestive of various idolatries and unworthy associations.

The only reason for creation given throughout Scripture is the *agape* of God. Creation is the manifestation of God's *agape*, of his glory, his beauty, his overflowing richness and generosity. Moreover, the present creation is only a beginning, *initium aliquod creaturae*.

The end to which creation leads is the realization of a union, in which nature and persons remain distinct, between man, the creature, made divine by grace but with his own consent and cooperation, and the One who, in the person of the Son, has taken upon himself human nature in order that we may become sharers in the divine nature, *consortes divinae naturae*. The key to biblical teaching, Jewish and Christian, about creation, in the end is only to be found in the doctrine that the creature is made godlike, what the Greek Fathers called *theiosis*.

As may be seen, such a doctrine of creation at once gives us an outlook, places us in a universe, in a world of thought, radically different from that to which Indian philosophies, or those of Plato or Spinoza, accustom us.

In metaphysical systems of these kinds man is part of the divine substance, or a mode of the divine substance. He is not a creature. The basic problem which arises is not: Why creation? but: Why the fall, why did each soul leave the divine unity, why exile and separation? To this question these metaphysical systems never make any answer except perhaps by a myth, the myth of an original failure, precosmic, responsible for the multiplication of beings, the individuation of souls, for space and time, matter and body. Instead of a metaphysic of creation we are presented with a metaphysic of fall and separation, up to the time of Hegel. In these circumstances salvation can only consist in returning to the original Unity, from which we have come forth and of which we are by nature members. Salvation consists in undoing the work of creation, or rather of the fall, in regaining the height from which the One was cast down to become many, the universal soul to become particular souls, eternity to become time, the spirit to become matter and nature. At the end of this cycle of events all will return to the One, unless the cycle is repeated for ever, as is taught by a number of such systems.

There is nothing of this kind in biblical thought. Creation is creation, and it is unique and irreversible. It is at the present moment, at the present moment of God's eternity, in the eternal noontide of his life, that God creates a being capable of sharing in the blessedness of his life. In order to create such a being, capable of becoming godlike, God creates a universe by its structure and natural evolution wholly designed for man. Fr Teilhard de Chardin wrote in 1918:

> After all, is not our Lord "mankind" or even "creation personified"? It is in the doctrine of divinization we may say that the key is found to creation. It is in Christ that the work is carried out of the divinization of human nature, of the whole of humanity which he takes to himself. That is why Christ is the head of all creation, the keystone of the great work. We see in the history of creation how all things are directed, little by little, towards the production of man. We see throughout Scripture how everything is directed little by little towards the manifestation of Christ.

In the eyes of Jews and Christians we are not by *nature* parts or modes of the divine substance. We do not come out of God; we are not drawn from his substance, born from him, consubstantial with God. We are creatures. Yet, though creatures, we are called to share in the personal life of God through a union which, in the words of Maurice Blondel, is an extension of the hypostatic union. Our deification is not a natural, original, fact from which we start; it is a process, a summons, a promise, a hope, a goal. It is not a question of our returning to our former state in the womb of the One (in the womb of the mother, as psychoanalysts would say when speaking of this myth), for we have never been in the One. We must toil, without any backward glance, towards that which lies ahead of us, like good athletes, as St Paul says, towards the goal, the Fullness.

Consequently theology, biblical, Jewish and Christian, involves, like metaphysics, a time structure radically different from that of the metaphysical system of India, or of Plato, Plotinus or Spinoza. The Christian looks at creation as irreversible in time, directed to a definite end, namely its divinization, and with no return. Plainly the Christian idea of time is not "linear", for time is not the same as space (cf. Bergson). We may call it "vectorial".

Here we have a starting point which is strictly metaphysical, organically joined with theology, and indeed with Christian mysticism, and which plays a central part, as we shall see.

The absolute, according to the Bible, Judaism, Christianity and Islam, is one. This gets rid of myths about warfare between gods, of which the ancient religions were full, as were later Gnostic sects. Nothing outside the absolute is uncreated or eternal, and in particular there is no pre-existing matter.

In Platonism and Gnosticism of the first centuries physical matter plays an ambiguous part. It bears the burden, and carries the responsibility, for all sins. In some Gnostic systems it is the principle and cause of evil. It represents a kind of anti-god, no less uncreated and eternal than the good.

In biblical theology and metaphysics there is nothing of this sort. Physical matter is created by God. The physical universe is the first thing to be created, and God declares that it is very beautiful and very good. Here again is a radical change of outlook. Matter is not the principle of evil. We shall have to seek elsewhere for the cause of evil.

So, too, according to Scripture man is created with a body.

There is no teaching about the pre-existence of the soul, nor is there any myth of the transmigration of souls from one body to another. There is no idea of a "fall" of the soul into the body, as we find described in the Upanishads, in Orphism, in Empedocles, Plato, Plotinus and all the Gnostic sects, up to and including the medieval Gnostic sects called "Catharists", and the philosophy of Schelling. Man is created with a bodily nature, and man, so created, is declared like all creation beautiful and good. Hence it is not the body which is responsible for evil.

Creation, the physical world of our senses, the body, are, in themselves and as created things, each excellent in its own order. There is no guilty rejection, in the biblical tradition, of the sensible, the bodily, the sexual; while in the Indian tradition, especially in Brahmanism, and in Platonism and Neoplatonism, matter, the body and sex are seen as deeply infected with guilt. It is an evil for the soul to have fallen into the body, to be attached to the body, and sex is the bond which attaches the soul to the body in a twofold way: first, in all of us it is the desire which binds us to matter, and, secondly, sex is the cause of procreation, that is, of the fall of fresh souls into bodies. Persuaded by this reasoning Manichees and Catharists forbade marriage, and especially the generation of children, since this casts down blessed souls into these bodies of clay and slime.

The biblical tradition is at the furthest possible remove from the hostility to natural bodily life. We shall see the consequences of this essentially optimistic and sane attitude when we consider the orthodox attitude to marriage.

If we analyse the inner structure and principles, whether implicit or explicit, in the tradition of biblical thought, we discover a certain number of views, theories, attitudes and assertions which can only be called metaphysical, because in all metaphysical writings of every age these questions have been regarded as belonging to metaphysics. We find in Scripture, explicitly and implicitly, a clear doctrine of being, of uncreated and of created being, of the distinction between the absolute and the world, a doctrine about matter, sense perception, soul and body; a doctrine, too, about freedom and conduct, thought and understanding. I have analysed and explained this doctrine elsewhere, and need not, therefore, return to the subject here.

I need only mention that this strictly metaphysical system, which is immanent, in an organically necessary way, in biblical theology, is a homogeneous system. The biblical teaching on freedom and evil is bound up with the teaching on creation, matter and the body. It is not the body or matter or the senses which are responsible for evil, but it is man himself who is responsible for the evil he does. That is the teaching of the great Jahvist theologian in the third chapter of Genesis, and in what follows. God created man for happiness and not for misery. Man's misery is not a necessity, a fatality, imposed on man by the structure of things, by creation, by nature. Man's misery is not part of God's plan; man himself causes his misery. The third chapter of Genesis, which speaks of the origin of mankind, speaks too, it seems to me, of the whole history of mankind. It is prophetic as well as historical, referring to the past and also the future. Through his own fault man left the paradise God had prepared for him; man was himself the cause of his downfall. It is not the gods (as in the cosmogonies of the ancient religions) who are responsible for man's misery. It is not a fatality due to the gods or to the stars. Human existence is not of itself an evil (as was taught by Brahmanism, Orphism and the Gnostics); above all bodily existence is not a misfortune, but quite the opposite, a wonderful creation.

The doctrine of freedom is taught throughout the Old Testament. We always find that the God of Israel respects the created freedom which he appeals to, anxiously and urgently, but which he never forces. A woman cannot be forced to give her love. This is impossible because love is only given freely. God cannot, and will not, force this freedom which he calls to the marriage union.

The New Testament did not change the metaphysical foundation whose structure can be seen in the Old Testament. We, too, always build on a metaphysic of creation. The doctrine of being—of the world, of man, of thought and conduct, and of freedom—is thus substantially the same as in the Old Testament. The writers of the New Testament are not aware of making any break with tradition in this respect. They feel that their work is one of fulfilment and completion. From the metaphysical standpoint the Christian doctrine of the Incarnation presents fresh problems, but it can only be understood within the biblical metaphysic of creation. In a universe of thought like that of Celsus, Plotinus or Porphyry (and later of Spinoza) the very idea of incarnation is meaningless, a contradiction in terms. The Intelligible, the divine, could not come and defile itself in the sensible, the material. The eternal could not enter into the temporal, the universal in the particular. It should be noticed that these metaphysical objections—repeated at the present day by philosophers of the Neoplatonic tradition, and also by some Jewish thinkers—depend on a certain number of metaphysical assumptions concerning nothing else than the intelligible and the sensible, the spiritual and the material, the divine and the human, the eternal and the temporal, the universal and the particular. Behind these objections and difficulties lies a hidden dualist assumption. If we accept the biblical approach, the approach of a metaphysic of immanence according to the tradition of biblical thought, the idea of incarnation does not involve these difficulties. The Lord can come into this world, which is his work, created in and through his word, and in which he continues to work up to the present day, and to the end of time. From the days of the Old Testament we find that the God of Israel "tabernacles" with his people. It is the Shekinah, the dwelling of God among his people. The creator God of Israel is transcendent of, and immanent in, the world. In him we are, and move, and live. He is at work not only in the continuous coming into being of the world, and the stars, and the growth of the vegetable order, but also in our conduct, thoughts, and acts of will (cf. Phil. 2. 13; Gal. 3. 5; Ephes. 3. 20; Col. 1. 29; 1 Cor. 3. 9).

The Incarnation, according to orthodox Christian theology, does not imply that God came into the sensible and material world and took to himself a human body, in the way that Zeus took the appearance of a man or an animal in order to go among men. The Incarnation in the view of the Church, as defined at the Council of Chalcedon, means that God is joined to a human nature, assumes a human nature, in a union wherein the necessary distinctions and the freedom of human nature are maintained. The Logos assumes a human nature, which freely consents to this deification. Thus Christ is the head of the new human race, which is made godlike in and through him. He is the seed from which springs this new, holy, human race, called to share in the very life of God.

It should be noticed in passing how many metaphysical problems are involved in this orthodox doctrine of the Incarnation, and how false philosophical assumptions, in regard, for instance, to anthropology, can cause fundamental errors as to the meaning of the Incarnation. From the standpoint of a dualist anthropology, for instance, there will be a tendency to think of the Incarnation as the taking of a body, as though the Logos took a human "body" without its free, rational, soul. That is the Apollinarian heresy.

These few remarks are only intended to show how Christian philosophical thought is rooted in traditional biblical thought, both Hebrew and of the New Testament. I have no wish to elaborate a long analysis, as has been done elsewhere. What should be noticed from the start is that Christian thought, theological as well as philosophical, has its origin in Scripture. Scripture is the supreme test of truth in all discussions with heretics. The first chapters of Genesis, the recital of creation, are the great foundation stone of Christian metaphysics, from the beginning, through the centuries, and at the present day. When Christian thought struggled with the Gnostics, it was the recital of creation to which it appealed in defence of the excellence of creation, of the natural world, of physical and bodily reality, of the unity of the one creator God. When the Fathers criticized Origen it was again in the name of the biblical doctrine of creation, and also of marriage, and of biblical anthropology. The account in Genesis was his strongest weapon when Augustine disputed with the Manichees. In the twelfth century against the Catharists, and in the nineteenth century against German idealism, when Catholic thought had to reformulate its own metaphysical principles, it was again the great priestly passage at the beginning of our Bibles which was appealed to and quoted, and which formed the touchstone of orthodox Christian metaphysics.

CHAPTER II

CREATION METAPHYSICS IN THE FIRST CHRISTIAN CENTURIES

In these pages I shall not deal in turn with each of the Fathers of the Church in the first Christian centuries. Such individual accounts already exist. I may mention, for example, Fr Cayré's *Manual of Patrology and the History of Theology*; the *Patrology* of J. Quasten, professor of early Church history and of Christian archaeology in the Catholic University of Washington, the *Histoire de la Littérature grecque chrétienne*, by Aimé Puech (*Les Belles Lettres*, 1928); the *Histoire de la Littérature latine chrétienne*, by Pierre de Labriolle (*ibid.*, 2nd ed., 1947); the *Patrology*, by Berthold Altaner.[1] In these works and in many others of the same kind there will be found a connected, historical, account of Christian patristic thought, a series of monographs devoted to each of the Fathers of the Church, with biographies, bibliographies and lists of the subjects peculiar to the thought of each. The works mentioned in the bibliographies give references to learned monographs devoted more especially to each of the Fathers of the Church.

[1] See Select Bibliography at the end of this volume.

I have not thought it necessary in these few pages to summarize the whole picture which they give of Christian thought in the first centuries. A summary would inevitably be so general that it would deprive Christian thought in the first centuries of its life, and hence of its interest. Consequently I have preferred another method. Instead of attempting a series of monographs, which others have done far better, I have chosen to take some fundamental problems of Christian thought in the first centuries and to trace out the kind of approach, formulation and solution adopted in regard to them. By this means I hope to show how in the first centuries of our era Christian thought, in certain fundamental metaphysical respects, approached its problems, what kind of system it evolved, what were its principles and its needs.

It should be noticed, too, before we embark on this analysis, that most histories of philosophy only devote one or two chapters to the period with which we are concerned. Emile Bréhier in his *Histoire de la Philosophie* (I, 2, ch. 8: "Hellénisme et Christianisme", p. 494) writes: "There was certainly not, in the first five centuries of our era, any specially Christian philosophy, involving a completely original scale of values, different from that of pagan thinkers." We shall see, and have already been able to suspect, that the truth is precisely the opposite: there exists an independent, original, Christian metaphysic, and Christian thought has been explicitly and formally aware of this. Bréhier, faithful to his principle that Christianity has no philosophic content of its own, devotes some thirty pages of his history to the period from St Paul to Pseudo-Denis (fifth century). In contrast to this Ueberweg devotes a whole volume to patristic and scholastic thought, the volume being completed by B. Geyer (*Grundriss der Geschichte der Philosophie*, II, *Die patristische und scholastische Philosophie*, 12th ed., Graz, 1951). From the beginning the author recognizes the strictly philosophical importance of Christianity:

> The coming of the Christian religion marks a decisive turning-point in the history of philosophy as well. What was new in religion became the starting point for a new stage in philosophy. Christianity made use, for the development and expression of its doctrinal content, of ancient philosophy. But this doctrinal content itself, its way of understanding God, the world—and man, is, nevertheless, fundamentally different from the attitude of antiquity. The reason for this is that every religion carries with it a doctrinal element. . . . That is why the development of philosophy has been influenced decisively by the Christian religion and by its development (*op. cit.*, p. 1).

Here we have precisely the opposite view to that of Bréhier.

Etienne Gilson in his *History of Christian Philosophy in the Middle Ages* devotes his first two chapters to the period we are considering. Jacques Chevalier, in his *Histoire de la Pensée* (vol. 2), also devotes a chapter to these first stages of Christian philosophy. And I may mention, too, that I have myself explained, in a book, *La métaphysique du christianisme et la naissance de la philosophie chrétienne* (Editions du Seuil, 1961), the chief points that show the gradual awareness among Christians of their own metaphysic in the first centuries.

The conception of God in patristic thought has been studied in a masterly fashion by G. L. Prestige in his book, *God in Patristic Thought* (new ed., London, 1952). The conception which Christian thought has formed of God is of course dependent on the doctrine of creation, and the reverse is also true. One of the most typical characteristics of the Jewish and Christian God is that he is creator. The conception of God thus depends, at least to some extent, on philosophy. This is the part of philosophy which has later been called natural theology.

We shall see throughout how the idea formed of the creation of man, the world, time—and, generally speaking, every metaphysical conception—involves a certain conception of God. It is always God who is to be found on the horizon of our analyses. It is in order to defend above all else a certain idea of God that Christian thought has, in the course of centuries, defended a certain idea of the relationship between God and the world, man, matter, time, human freedom, human nature and reason. Here I shall not be directly concerned with the Christian conception of God in the first centuries of patristic thought, because a study of this kind is more suitable in a strictly theological context.

THE ASSERTION OF CREATION

The doctrine of creation, which is connected essentially with the Jewish and Christian doctrine about God, is taught explicitly in many passages of the New Testament: Mark 10. 6; 13. 19; Matt. 19. 4; Rom. 1. 20; Ephes. 3. 19; Col. 1. 16; Apoc. 4. 11; 10. 6, etc.

From the beginning of Christianity it is a constant and fundamental doctrine. "The first thing of all [we read in the Shepherd of Hermas (*Commandments*, 1, 11)] is: believe that there is but one God, who has created all and set it in order, who has made everything pass from nothing to being, who upholds everything, and alone is upheld by nothing."[2] God, writes Aristides (*Apologia*), is without beginning and eternal, immortal and needing nothing, while the elements themselves are not gods; they are corruptible and subject to change; they have been produced out of not being by a commandment of him who is truly God, who is incorruptible and unchangeable and invisible. Christians know God as the creator and fashioner of the universe, and they worship no other God than him. We see from this

[2] I give here short references. For more detail, for a fuller explanation of the texts, for the original Latin or Greek, the reader is referred to my book: *La métaphysique du christianisme et la naissance de la philosophie chrétienne*, Paris, éditions du Seuil, 1961.

passage how the fathers criticized the divinization of the world and of the elements by the pagan philosophers. We shall find this criticism frequently repeated.

Justin mentions the doctrine of creation: "The Hebrew prophets", he writes, "have glorified the author of the universe as God and father" (*Dialogue with Tryphon*, 7, 1). "We think that the God who has created all is above this changing nature" (*1st Apology*, 20). "God", writes Tatian, "is spirit. He is not immanent in matter, but is the creator of spirits, of matter and forms, which are in it. We know him by his creation, and we conceive of his invisible power by his works. I will not worship his creation, which he has made for our benefit" (*Speech to the Greeks*, 4). "We distinguish God from matter", writes Athenagoras; "we show that matter and God are distinct, and that there is a great difference between them, for the divine is uncreated, eternal, apparent only to spirit and reason, while matter is created and corruptible. Our doctrine declares one God only, creator of this universe" (*Supplicatio*, 4).

We distinguish, continues Athenagoras, and we separate the uncreated and the created. We do not consider stones and wood, gold and silver, as gods. Undoubtedly the world is beautiful. Nevertheless we must not worship the world, but its maker. Further on Athenagoras states that God is free in creating; the world was not made because God had need of it. For God exists entirely for himself. I do not abandon God in order to worship the elements, to which nothing is possible except what is ordained for them. If, while admiring the beauty of the heavens and the elements I do not worship them as gods, because I know the reason for their dissolution, how could I call those things gods which I know that men have made? Every one of those beings to which divine essence has been attributed has had a beginning. So, too, Theophilus of Antioch says: "Unlike pagan philosophers we recognize God, but only one God, creator, author, and governor of all this universe" (*Ad Autolycum,* 3, 9). God is founder and creator, because he has produced and created all things. He has made the heavens; the earth is his work; the sea is his creation; he has formed man in his own image. The universe has been created by God, drawn out of nothing into existence, so that by his works we should know and realize his greatness (*ibid.,* 1, 4). In his *Proof of the Apostolic Preaching* Irenaeus writes:

> God is the eternal being, above all created things; all is set beneath him, and it is God who has created all. Of necessity the things created here below draw from some cause the principle of their existence, and the principle of all things is God. For he himself has been created by no one, but by him all has been created. So this is how the Christian teaching should be expressed: one God, the uncreated father, creator of the universe, above whom there is no other God, and beside whom there is no other God. One God, creator of the universe: this is the very first article of our faith.

The author of the *Elenchos,* or refutation of all the heresies, formerly identified with Origen, and then, in the nineteenth century, with Hippolytus, but more recently, by M. Pierre Nautin, with a certain Josephus, after having explained the teaching of the Greek philosophers about the world and its origin, concludes: "They all came down from the divine so as to be involved in things which are in a state of becoming. Struck with the greatness of creation they thought that it was the divine. They gave the preference, one to this part of creation and one to that, but they did not recognize the God of these creatures who made them" (1, 26, 3). The author of the Epistle to Diognetus states that creation has been brought about by the Word: "It is the almighty himself, the creator of all things, the invisible, God himself, who, sending him from the height of heaven, has set among men the truth, the holy Word. Through him God has created the heavens" (7, 2).

Clement of Alexandria criticizes the way in which the pagan philosophers take the elements, the stars and the world to be divine:

> Some have somehow gone so far wrong as to worship, not God, but a divine work, the sun, the moon, the whole choir of the stars: against all reason they think of them as gods.... On this point all the learned philosophers are mistaken, recognizing that man is truly born for the contemplation of heavenly things, but worshipping heavenly phenomena, and the spectacle presented to their eyes.... Let no one of you worship the sun, but let him turn his desire towards the sun's maker: let him not regard the world as divine, but seek the creator of the world (*Protrepticus*, 4, 63).

And Clement criticizes Aristotle for not knowing creation: "The father of the school (the Peripatetics), instead of conceiving the father of the universe, believes that he whom he calls 'most high' is the soul of all; that is to say, he contradicts himself by regarding the soul of the world as god" (*ibid.*, 5, 64, 4). We shall also find in St Augustine, Lactantius and others, this criticism of the idea that God is the soul of the world, or that the soul of the world is god. Celsus had claimed in his *True Word* that the Jews worship the heavens. Origen had no difficulty in replying that Celsus was wrong in this. For, adds Origen, in his book against Celsus, it is quite clear to anyone who has studied the doctrines of Judaism, that the Jews who are faithful to their law worship only the God who has created the heavens and all things. Neither Jews nor Christians say that the heavens are god, unlike the Greeks who say that the whole universe is god, the first god according to the Stoics, the second god according to certain Platonic philosophers, the third god according to others (5, 6, 7). We Christians adore neither angels, nor the sun, nor the moon, nor the stars, nor what the Greeks call visible or sensible gods. These cults are pagan; but are not practised by that holy and chosen race, that kingdom of priests which is the Hebrew people (5, 10).

According to Methodius of Olympus God is the almighty, the Father and creator of the universe (*The Banquet*, 2, 7; *de creatis*, 3, 11).

Eusebius of Caesarea, in the *Preparatio Evangelica*, criticizes the way in which the pagan nations make gods of the elements of the world, the stars and men themselves. In Book VII, Eusebius comes to the "philosophy of the Hebrews". The Hebrews, he writes, are the first and only people who have, through rational thought, judged that the primary elements of the world, earth, water, air, fire, of which this universe is made up, and the sun, moon, and stars are not gods but the works of God. They have seen that bodily substance, of its nature, is not only without reason, but also without soul. They have understood that the order of the universe, which is governed in a wise and happy way, filled with living beings, endowed with reason and not so endowed, cannot be attributed to a mechanical cause. They have worshipped the creator of all things (7, 3).

Athanasius of Alexandria, at the beginning of his *Explanation of the Faith*, expresses himself thus: "We believe in one God, unbegotten, almighty father, creator of all things visible and invisible" (*Expositio fidei*, 1).

St Aphraates in his turn formulates the faith of the Church as follows: "We ought to believe in God, Lord of all things, who has created the heavens and the earth and the sea and all the beings that are in them, who has created men to his own image . . . " (*Homilies*, 1, 19).

"Those ignorant of God's existence," writes Basil of Caesarea, "have not admitted that a reasonable cause has governed the coming into being of the universe. They have not known: 'In the beginning God made heaven and earth.' That is why they have believed that the universe of beings was without guide or governor, but was carried along by chance" (*Homilies on the Hexaemeron*, 1, 2).

St Augustine, in his great book, *The City of God*, criticizes the pantheism of ancient philosophy: "We worship God, not the heavens or the earth, nor the soul or the souls scattered throughout living things. We worship God who has made the heavens and the earth and all that they contain, who has made all souls" (*De Civ. Dei*, 7, 29).

So, too, Lactantius, in his *Institutions*, criticized the treating of the stars and the elements of the world as gods by the pagan philosophers and poets (2, 5–6).

When Christian thought criticized the deification of the elements, the stars and the universe, that is, ancient panpsychism and pantheism, it carried on the movement of Hebrew biblical thought, and left ample scope for the idea of creation, that is, for the distinction between the absolute and the world, and for the recognition of the relation between God and the world as that of a gift.

CREATION AND FASHIONING: THE IDEA OF MATTER, AND THE PROBLEMS INVOLVED

When criticizing the deification of the stars, of supernatural forces and elements, as well as ancient panpsychism, the Fathers of the Church picked up the thread of a tradition running back to the prophets of Israel. The prophets, indeed, had often and vigorously criticized the way in which the ancient religions regarded the world as sacred and divine. As I have already said, biblical thought presents itself as striving to be rational and free from myth. Christian thought continues this effort to foster reason and get rid of myth. That is why, in this sphere, it deserves to be called philosophy.

The problem of matter provides Christian thought with the opportunity to clarify its notion of creation, and its teaching both about being and about evil.

We know that in the ancient mythologies, Assyro-Babylonian as well as Indian and Hellenic, chaos precedes the formation of the world. Chaos comes first. It is from a pre-existing chaos that the demiurge or the god fashions or sets in order the world. In fact it is thus the chaos which is the absolute, the first principle, the eternal uncreated. The gods in these mythologies often issue from the chaos by a tragic theogony. We find stories of this kind in the theosophical speculations which lie at the source of many institutions in German thought.

The Hebrew theologians had rejected all this mythology, and, in the first account of creation at the beginning of the Bible, which is, according to biblical criticism, the work of a school of theologians of the fifth or fourth century B.C., God comes first: "At the beginning God created . . .". There remain in Scripture traces of the ancient mythology attributing to the chaos a dangerous reality which the good god must master, but these traces are no more, in the Bible, than images and folklore stories. No theological or metaphysical importance is any longer attributed to them.

In the teaching about matter, which develops in various forms in Plato, Aristotle and Plotinus, there seem to remain elements derived from these ancient mythologies. Matter, according to Plato, is a fundamental disorder which has been controlled and overcome, like the chaos of Hesiod. The disorder comes first. Then comes order, but it continues eternally to be threatened by this primitive and original disorder, which is the cause of evil in the world. We can see how the teaching about matter comes to be bound up with a particular teaching about evil.

With Aristotle the notion of matter is more empirical and less mythological. A vessel is made up of matter and form. The matter is the marble, the form is given by the artist. Thus all concrete things are constituted of matter and a form. Man himself is made up of matter informed by a soul. If we apply this empirical analysis, derived from experience in fashioning things, to creation as a whole—something, of course, which Aristotle did not do—the result would be to describe God as fashioning the world, and giving a form to pre-existing matter.

Christian thought has reacted against such theories, and has plainly recognized the distinction which exists between creating and fashioning. Matter, according to Christian theology and metaphysics, is not a primitive, uncreated, reality, coeternal with the creation god, and used by the creation god for the purpose of fashioning the world. "Matter," writes Tatian, "is not without any external principle, as God is, and, since it is not without such a principle, it has not the same power as God. It has been created, it is the work of another, and it could only have been produced by the creator of the universe" (*Oratio adversus Graecos*, 5). Theophilus of Antioch criticizes Plato explicitly on this question:

As to Plato and his followers, they recognize a god, un-created, father, and author of the universe; then we find the view that matter, like God, has no beginning, that it develops together with God! If God has no beginning, and matter has no beginning, God is no longer author of the universe according to the Platonic school, and the absolute sovereignty of God is no longer proved, if we listen to them. Moreover, if God, having no beginning, can suffer no change, matter, if it has no beginning, will be equally unchangeable, and the equal of God. . . . Why should it be surprising, if God had drawn the world out of pre-existing matter? A human work-man, when given matter, does with it all that he wishes. But the power of God is shown just in his starting with nothing, in order to do all that he wills. Man can make statues; but he cannot give to the work of his hands the power of speech or of life or of sensation. God is greater than him in this power to make beings who can reason, live, and have con-sciousness (*Ad Autolycum*, 2, 4).

Theophilus of Antioch also criticizes the cosmogonic poem of Hesiod:

> In some sense he supposes, as a hypothesis, matter and the creation of the world, when he says, "At first there was chaos, and then the earth, opening wide its womb ... and so on." By these statements he has not shown us by what means they have come into being. For, if at first there was chaos, if matter already existed, and was unbegotten, who was it who prepared, governed and carried out this transformation? Is it matter itself which is transformed, and becomes the world? For Zeus was born very long after, not only matter, but also the world, indeed after many men—and also his father, Cronos. Was there not, rather, a sovereign principle which was his creator? I mean God, who made him (*ibid.*, 2, 6). [With the Hellenic cosmogony Theophilus of Antioch contrasts the teaching of the Hebrew prophets:] But the men of God, who received what the Holy Ghost gave them, the prophets, having inspiration and wisdom from God himself, were taught by God and were holy and just. They were, moreover, judged worthy, as a reward, to be the instruments of God, and to share in his wisdom; it is through the influence of this wisdom that they spoke of the creation of the world, and of all the rest.... In the first place they have agreed in teaching us that God created all things out of nothing. There has been nothing which developed together with God; he depends on nothing, he is conscious of no need, he comes before the ages (*ibid.*, 2, 9, 10).

The Pseudo-Justin makes a clear distinction between creation, which is strictly God's work, and fashioning, which is man's work, and states this again in reference to Plato. "I think," writes the unknown author, "that we should notice the following. Plato does not call God creator (*poieten*) but demiurge (*demiurgon*) of the gods. There is a great difference between these two notions, even in Plato's view. The creator, indeed, has no need of anything, and it is of his own power and will that he creates what is created; the demiurge gets from matter the power to carry out his work, and thus he governs what comes into being . . ." (*Cohortatio ad Graecos*, 22).

St Irenaeus, in a fragment which has been preserved (fragment 34), returns to the distinction between divine creation and human fashioning. Some people, he writes, moved by a strange kind of spirit, deny to God half of his creative power, saying that God is the cause only of the quality conveyed to the matter, and claiming that matter itself is produced from nothing. In his great book against heresy Irenaeus expresses the distinction between creation and fashioning as follows: "Men can certainly never make things out of nothing; they need to be provided with matter. But God is greater than man, in so far as the matter, which he fashions, though it did not exist previously, he himself creates" (*Adv. Haer.*, 2, 10, 4).

Certain Gnostic or theosophical sects, from the earliest Christian days, have taken the doctrine of eternal, uncreated matter from ancient mythologies. Thus Hermogenes, as Tertullian tells us, supposes the existence of uncreated matter, which he described as like the uncreated God, making it a kind of goddess-mother of the elements. Tertullian devoted a whole book to the refutation of the dualism of Hermogenes. In this book Tertullian shows the power and penetration of his reasoning. He criticizes the system of Hermogenes as inconsistent, and exhibits its contradictions. I have given an account of his argument.[3] The theory of uncreated, evil matter has been devised for nothing else than to justify God and to give an explanation of evil. But, adds Tertullian, this theory gives us no help. Indeed the theory of uncreated matter, coeternal with God and responsible for evil, destroys the very notion of an almighty God, It is implied polytheism.

The author of the *Elenchos* against all the heresies, formerly attributed to Origen, then to Hippolytus of Rome, and recently by M. Nautin to Josephus, a Christian, also criticizes

[3] *La métaphysique du christianisme* . . . , pp. 119–128.

the theory of Hermogenes, underlining its resemblance to the theory of Plato.

A certain Hermogenes, wishing to invent something new, taught that God made the world out of a matter which was coeternal and uncreated: for, said he, God can only make the beings he makes with that which exists.... This matter, eternally swept along in a wild and disordered movement, is controlled by God in the following way: seeing it bubbling like a molten metal, he divided it into two; taking one part he calmed its wild nature, leaving the other part with its disorderly movement. The part under control, according to Hermogenes, is the universe. The other part remains wild, and is called disorderly matter.... This absurdity comes from Socrates, and has been developed by Plato better than by Hermogenes (*Elenchos*, 8, 17).

We recognize in the theory as worked out by Hermogenes the ancient cosmogonic myths, which we find described in the Egyptian and Assyro-Babylonian religious writings, and later in the theology of Hesiod. Myths have a long life.

With the teaching of Plato and the dualists the author of the *Elenchos* contrasts the Christian teaching:

There is one God who is first and only God, creator and lord of all things. There was nothing at the beginning with him, neither infinite chaos, nor measureless sea, nor firm land, nor dense air, nor hot fire, nor light spirit, nor blue vault of the wide heavens; but he was alone.... When he willed, he made things, which did not exist before he willed to make them. ... It is because they knew nothing (of the causes) that the Greeks glorified in their graceful way the parts of creation, and had no knowledge of the Creator. They provided a starting point for the heresiarchs (*Elenchos*, 7, 29).

The real Hippolytus, author of a book against all the heresies, a fragment of which has been edited by M. P. Nautin, expresses the same idea in almost the same terms. But he introduces some thoughts about the part played by the Logos in creation: "God, who existed by himself and with whom there was nothing at the beginning, willed to create the world. By his Understanding, his Will, and his Word, he made the world.... There was nothing at the beginning with God" (*Against all the Heresies*, fragment).

Origen teaches plainly that matter was created by God, and did not exist before him. He criticizes those who state against this that matter is uncreated and writes:

> We believe that God created things out of nothing, and not out of pre-existing matter (*In Ioannem comm.*, 1, 17). If anyone doubts that God could form the world without pre-existing, uncreated matter, because a human workman could not do so, because a maker of statues needs metal, a carpenter wood, a mason stone, we ask him if he believes God can carry out all his design without meeting with hindrances or obstacles. In virtue of his power and of his ineffable wisdom God can form as he chooses those qualities which will adorn the universe. In the same way his will must be able to produce the very substance which it needs. To those who would maintain the contrary we should say: God, according to your theory, has certainly been very fortunate in finding ready for him an uncreated substance without which he would not be able to be either demiurge or father or benefactor or good, and would not have possessed the corresponding attributes. But who has so arranged pre-existing matter that it is exactly right for the formation of the universe as it exists? Are we to suppose a providence previous to God, which would have provided him with the matter, and made it possible that the skill of the great craftsman should not be wasted, as would have happened had there been no substance from which he could produce the beauties of the world? (*Commentary on Genesis*, preserved by Eusebius of Caesarea, *Preparatio Evangelica*, 7, 20).

In his *Homilies on Genesis* Origen sums up the points on which Greek philosophy disagrees with Christian philosophy as follows:

> Many philosophers hold that there is only one God, creator of all things; and in this they are in agreement with God's

law. Some have even added that God has made all things, and that he directs all by his Word, and that it is the Word of God that governs all. In this they are in agreement, not only with the law, but also with the Gospels. What is called moral and natural philosophy agrees almost wholly with what we think. But it disagrees with us when it says that matter is coeternal with God, when it maintains that God is not concerned with corruptible things, that his providence is reserved for the spaces of the heavens, when it holds that man's life depends on the course of the stars, when it says that this world will last for ever and have no end. And there are many other points, too, on which the upholders of this philosophy are either in agreement or disagreement with us (*op. cit.*, 14, 3).

Methodius of Olympus, in his dispute with a Gnostic dualist, states an argument which may be found also in the *Preparatio Evangelica* of Eusebius under the name of Maximus: "I think that you, too, will not fail to recognize that two uncreated principles cannot possibly exist together...." There follows a piece of dialectic aimed at showing the inconsistency of the dualist theory (*Treatise on Free Will*, 5). At the end of the treatise, in the form of a dialogue, Methodius makes the orthodox speaker formulate the Christian teaching:

Do not say that anything exists of itself, and was at the beginning with God; do not seek to deny him the power which is his greatest attribute. It is he who has given existence to all things. They did not exist before that, and they do not possess an existence without a beginning. Why do you wish God to be only a craftsman? Why underrate his kindness, as though he had only improved matter by his art, and had not also given it existence? There could be nothing which existed with God at the beginning.... He is not only creator of forms, nor has he mingled his substance with another substance, for he is himself the creator of all substances (*ibid.*, 21).

Let no one ask [writes Lactantius] from what material God has created his great and wonderful works. For he created all out of nothing. We must not listen to the poets, who claim that at the beginning there was chaos, that is to say, things and elements confused together, and that only afterwards did God set in order and adorn the world he has constituted. It is easy to reply that they have not understood the power of God, since they believe that God can do nothing unless he starts with a matter ready to his hand. That is an error into which the philosophers have fallen (*Divine Institutions*, 2, 8).

In Book VII of the *Preparatio Evangelica* Eusebius of Caesarea treats of the problem of the eternity of matter. Hebrew thought teaches that the creator of all things is one, the God who is creator, too, of that substance of which bodies are constituted, and which the Greeks call *hule.* Barbarians and Greeks teach theories opposed to this teaching of the Bible. Some claim that matter is uncreated and the source of evil; others that matter, which of its own nature is without quality or form, has received order and qualities through the power of God (*op. cit.*, 7, 18). Eusebius, making use of the writings of his predecessors, criticizes at length this dualism of principles.

Athanasius of Alexandria lays the blame directly on Plato.

There have been many different explanations of the production of the world and the creation of the universe, and each has been a different one. Some say that everything came into being of itself and by chance....

Others, among them Plato, who is so eminent among the Greeks, say that it is out of pre-existing and uncreated matter that God made the world; God could have produced nothing, if this matter had not already existed, just as wood must exist before the carpenter, if he is to work with it. Those who speak in this way do not realize that they attribute a lack of power to God. For, if he is not himself the cause of matter, but produces everything entirely from pre-existing matter, he shows a lack of power, since without matter he cannot produce any created thing.... How can we call him creator and demiurge, if he relies on something else, namely matter, for the possibility of creation? Otherwise God would only be, in their view, the craftsman and not the creator who gives being, if he works with already existing matter, and is not himself its cause. In short, he cannot be called creator, if he does not create the matter from which creatures are derived. . . . These are their myths. But the teaching inspired by God and the faith according to Christ reject this vain reasoning as atheistic doctrine. . . . It is not out of pre-existing matter, but out of nothing, that God has created all things (*Oratio de incarnatione Verbi*, 2–3).

So, too, St Basil, in his *Homilies on the Hexaemeron*, criticizes the teaching that matter is uncreated. What has deceived the philosophers, writes Basil, is that with us, men, the craftsman uses pre-existing matter, wood or iron. But God is not a human craftsman. He produces the matter which he goes on to use. God does not merely devise forms. He creates the very nature of things (*op. cit.*, 2, 2).

Henceforth this became an accepted teaching in Christian thought, and we find it expressed by Gregory of Nyssa, Epiphanius, Ambrose of Milan, Augustine, Theodoret of Cyrus, and John Damascene. Christian thought has come to realize explicitly a metaphysical distinction between creation and fashioning, between the work of God and the work of man. St Thomas Aquinas, who sums up all the positive achievement of patristic tradition, states this conclusion, when he writes that the act of creation belongs to God alone, *solius Dei est creare*.

When they distinguished between God's act of creation and man's act of fashioning, the Fathers reached a fresh idea of matter. Matter is not an uncreated substance, eternal, coeternal with God, opposed to God, which the demiurge struggles with in order to carry out his work. Matter is not the principle of evil. Matter is created, and is good in its own order. It has not that almost divine dignity, that wicked power, which the Gnostics and Manichaeans attributed to it. We must look elsewhere than in matter and in the many for the principle and cause of evil. Christian thought has made a clear distinction between the problem of evil and the ontology of matter. From the standpoint of reason this is a great advance.

THE ABSOLUTE IS ONE, AND IS THE CREATOR

We have just seen how Christian thought from the first centuries has rejected the teaching that matter is an uncreated principle. This teaching, which is derived from the ancient mythologies and cosmogonies of the oriental religions, had left traces in the philosophy of Plato. The Gnostics of the first centuries of our era gave the teaching of the two principles a sharper, indeed tragic, form. Here I need not discuss the different Gnostic systems which developed in the first centuries. A volume of the present series has been devoted to that subject. All that I need do is to say quite simply that, from the metaphysical point of view, which is our concern here, two leading types may be distinguished: 1. A radically dualist type. At the beginning there were two principles, one good and the other evil. The good principle is the god who is a stranger and unknown. The evil principle is creator of the world and of bodies. Matter and body are its work. 2. A second type of Gnosticism is more developed. The world is created by an evil demiurge, but he is derived by a theogonic process, so to speak, from an absolute principle. Matter and body are the work of the lower god, who is identified with the God of the Old Testament. The cosmogony comes at the end of a theogonic process. In the two types this material world is not the work of a single, good God, the God of Abraham, Isaac and Jacob. There are two principles, and the God of the Old Testament is identified with the lower or evil principle. We can see how this ontological dualism and this Gnostic theosophy were at the root of an anti-Semitism, an anti-Judaism, which from Marcion to Fichte, Hegel and Simone Weil, were to have many offspring. This material world, this bodily creation around us, were not held to be the work of the one God, the God of Abraham and of Jesus, but the work of a lower or evil principle. This being so the present world can tell us nothing about the one God, the God of Abraham, since this world is not his work. We see, too, how the rejection of natural, rational knowledge of God drawn from creation is perhaps partly derived from assumptions of a dualist kind. A certain manner of approach, like that of Karl Barth with his idea of God as "wholly other", completely severs the relation between God and his creation, and makes it impossible to understand how creation manifests its Creator, and teaches us about him.

Christian thought from its beginning has been constantly confronted with a dualism which is always rearing its head. It is the oneness of God the creator which has been in question, the excellence of creation, the whole of Christian theology and metaphysics.

Irenaeus approves of what Justin says: "I should not believe the Lord himself, if he told us of a God who was not the Creator" (*Adversus haereses*, 4, 6, 2). "The Church, though spread over the whole habitable world to its furthest confines, unanimously holds the faith, received from the apostles and their disciples, in one God, the almighty Father, who has created heaven and earth and the waters and all that is in them" (*op. cit.*, 1, 10, 1). "It is the extreme of wickedness to say that the Creator of heaven and earth, the one, only, almighty God, above whom there is no other God, has been produced by a failure, a fall, this failure being itself produced from another failure, in such a way that, as these heretics think, the creator would be the result of a third failure" (1, 16, 3). In their blasphemous wickedness they call him "fruit of a fall" (1, 19, 1). "We hold firmly to the rule of truth," writes Irenaeus; "there is one God alone, who has created all by his Logos, who has set all in order, and has made it out of nothing.... It is he who has made the world, it is he who has formed man, it is he, the God of Abraham, the God of Isaac, and the God of Jacob, above whom there is no other God, nor Principle, nor Power, nor Fullness; it is he, the Father of our Lord, Jesus Christ" (1, 22, 1).

Irenaeus directed his critical analysis in particular upon Valentinian Gnosticism. Tertullian, again, devoted a whole book to the refutation of Marcion, who, as we know, taught two uncreated and eternal principles, one good and the other evil. The evil principle was supposed to have created the world. This theory aimed at explaining evil. Tertullian analyses the teaching of Marcion, and, as with Hermogenes, shows up its contradictions by a vigorous and penetrating process of reasoning. To the teaching of Marcion Tertullian opposes, as did Irenaeus, the "rule of faith": "The rule of faith, which is indivisible and which alone is unalterable and irreformable, consists in believing in one God, almighty and creator of the world, in Jesus Christ his son, and so on" (*De virg. vel.*, 1).

Origen, in his book on the Principles, states the first article of the Christian faith: "One God, who has created all, and set it in order...; God of Abraham and of the twelve Patriarchs, of Moses and of the prophets, God of Jesus the Christ, God both just and good, God of the Old and of the New Testament" (*De principiis*, 1, Preface, 4). In the commentary which he wrote on the epistle of St Paul to Titus, Origen states his idea of heresy as follows: "We call all those heretics, however different may be the fables they invent to clothe their dreams, who, while professing to believe in Christ, hold that the God of the Law and the prophets is other than the God of the Gospel and the Father of our Lord Jesus Christ, such are the followers of Marcion, Valentinus, Basilides, and those who are called Sethians. . . ."

The Council of Nicaea, in its first article, is not aimed directly at polytheism, but at the dualism of principles which is a modified form of polytheism. The Council of Nicaea, together with the whole Christian tradition which preceded it, asserts the oneness of God, Creator and Father of all things: "We believe in one only God, Father almighty, creator of all things, visible and invisible...."

Henceforth it is an accepted doctrine, defined and explicitly formulated by the thought of the Church. Later, against the Manichees, orthodox Christian thought had to return to this assured belief, and to assert it against the Manichaean heretics who once again called it in question. Thus, in the fourth century, St Ephrem wrote a number of sermons against Marcion and Mani, and a hymn in refutation of their theories. Cyril of Jerusalem, in his catechetical treatise, sets out the same basic view:

> First, in order that the teaching about God may be established as a firm basis for your mind: God is one, unbegotten, without cause or beginning, unchangeable, unalterable.... If you hear a heretic say that the just God is other than the good God, remember at once that this is the poisoned arrow of heresy. For some have impiously dared to divide the one God by their words; and some have said that the creator and master of the soul is other than the creator of the body, thus teaching a doctrine which is both unreasonable and sacrilegious. The God who is creator of souls and bodies is one. The demiurge of heaven and earth, the creator of angels and archangels is one (*Catecheses*, 4).

Augustine, who spent nine years as a Manichee, afterwards engaged in a long struggle with the heresy of Mani. We shall return to his dispute when we come to the problems of anthropology.

THE FREEDOM OF THE CREATOR: CREATION IS A GIFT

According to some ancient and modern theosophical systems, creation is a necessary phase in the coming into being of the absolute; cosmogony is theogony; the coming into being of the world is imposed on the absolute by necessity, either internal or external, by a need for development or by the requirements of its gradual process of awareness. Orthodox Christian thought has rejected all these theogonic notions. Creation is a gift, creation is grace, creation is the first grace. The absolute is *agape*. Creation is the work, the expression, of God's *agape*. By its rejection of the theogonic myths involved in the Gnostic speculations, from Valentinus to Hegel, orthodox Christian thought has guarded its idea of God.

God, writes Athenagoras, did not make man because he had any need to do so, for his own benefit, since he needs nothing (*De resurrectione mortuorum*, 12).

Irenaeus, in his controversy with the Gnostics, insisted on this freedom of God in creating. It is not, he writes, because God is moved by another, but as a result of his own free decision, that God has created all things, since he is the one God, the one Lord (*Adv. hær.*, 2, 1, 1). He has acted freely, of himself, in virtue of his own power, and has set in order and perfected all things (2, 30, 9). He has need of nothing, and is self-sufficient (3, 8, 3). In the beginning it was not because God needed man that he created Adam, but in order to have someone to whom he could communicate his gifts. For God was not previous to Adam only, but to all creatures; the Logos glorified the Father, dwelling in him, and the Logos was himself glorified by the Father, as he said himself (John 17, 5), (4, 14, 1). The absolute, who is one, is not alone before creation takes place. He does not need creation in order to become conscious of himself, by contrast with a non-ego, as Fichte said, or, as in Hegel's view, by alienating himself in nature. The theology of the Trinity gives assurance of the freedom of the act of creation and of its character as a favour given. This idea was to be taken up by St Thomas Aquinas (*Summa Theol.* I, qu. 32, art. 1, ad tertium).

So, too, Hilary of Poitiers says: "God did not create man because he had any need of his help in any way but because he is good. He created man such that man is capable of sharing in God's own beatitude, and he perfected him with rational life, giving him life and understanding, so as to be able to communicate to him his own eternity" (*Tractatus super psalmos*, 2, 15).

Basil of Caesarea criticizes the Neoplatonic idea which sees in the production of the many from the one, of the sensible world from the intelligible, only a necessary and involuntary emanation, as the body produces the shadow, or burning fire brightness, or ice cold:

> Because many of those, who have conceived the world as existing with God from all eternity, refuse to believe that it is his work, but say that it was necessarily present as the shadow of his power (they admit, indeed, that God is cause of the world, but consider him an involuntary cause, as the body is of its shadow, fire of its light), the prophet, Moses, in order to correct such an error, declared, in terms that were quite precise, "In the beginning God created". He did not say that God was of necessity cause of being, but that he created out of his goodness this valuable work, out of his wisdom this beautiful work, out of his power this mighty work (*Homilies on the Hexaemeron*, 1).

Augustine, when commenting on the beginning of Genesis, in *The City of God*, states the same conclusions: "By these words, God saw that it was good, is declared plainly enough that God from no necessity, or need to satisfy any purpose of his own, but simply out of his goodness, created what has been made, because this was good ..." (*De civitate Dei*, 11, 24). So, too, in his commentary on the psalms, Augustine expresses the same traditional idea: "God was not forced to create anything he created, but he created whatever he willed. The cause of all that he created is his will. ... God created out of goodness; he had no need of any of the things he created" (*Ennar. in Psalm.*, 134, 10).

CREATION AND GENERATION

In the ancient mythologies of the Egyptian and Assyro-Babylonian religions, as in those of Orphism, the creation of gods and of the world was represented as the result of a process in which wicked deeds mingled with acts of generation. Finally, man was created from the seed or the spittle of a god, and was derived from the god's substance. The Hebrew theologians, who composed the recitals of creation which we find at the beginning of our Bibles, reacted strongly against these mythologies: man was not created out of the god's substance; he was created to the image and likeness of God, which is quite different.

The Gnostic mythologies of the first Christian centuries often reproduced these ancient ideas. Christian thought had to rid the orthodox conception of creation of these Gnostic intrusions. It did so in two fields.

Arianism, as shown in the description of it given by the Fathers, regarded the Logos once again as a creature, and hence reduced the generation of the Word to nothing more than an act of creation. The Fathers, especially St Athanasius, reacted against this reduction of the generation of the Word to an act of creation, and thus emphasized the fundamental distinction which exists between creation and generation.

The Manichaean mythology, like the ancient eastern mythologies, also conceived the creation of the world and of men as the result of a series of catastrophes and of unions. Man was thought to have been produced by a series of falls and of monstrous unions. In the Manichaean system the human soul is ultimately a part of the divine substance, separated, exiled, in an evil matter. Against this mythology Augustine asserted the distinction which exists between creation and generation: according to orthodox Christianity, the human soul is not a part of the divine substance, for it has not been generated by God, but created. The human soul is not consubstantial with God, while, on the other hand, the Word is consubstantial with God the Father, for it is generated and not created. We see how, in two different fields, orthodox Christian thought recognized the same fundamental metaphysical distinction between creation and generation. We may notice here how the question is presented in the first of these two fields, that of the struggle against the Arian heresy.

In a passage on the decrees of the council of Nicaea, Athanasius the Great quotes a letter of Denis, bishop of Rome, in which the distinction between creation and generation is already shown:

> We must not say that the Logos of God is something made or created, but that it is generated from the substance of the Father. This Denis, bishop of Rome, declared: "No less must those be blamed who think that the Son is something made, and who suppose that the Lord came into being like one of those things which have been created. For Scripture bears witness that generation is in harmony with what he is, and is fitting to him, but not the act of fashioning nor creation. Thus it is blasphemous, not slightly but in the highest degree, to say that the Lord is in any sense created. For, if the Son came into being, there was a time when he did not exist" (*De decretis Nic. syn.*, 26, 1–4).

To the Arian theory, as they understood it, the Fathers opposed the orthodox Christian doctrine. Thus Alexander of Alexandria, in his letter to Alexander of Thessalonica, says: "We believe in one Father, unbegotten . . . and in one Lord, Jesus Christ, the only begotten Son of God, begotten, not of nothing, but of the Father. . . ."

The Council of Antioch in 325 states the same distinction: "Faith . . . in one God, the almighty Father, creator of heaven and earth . . . and in one Lord, Jesus Christ, only begotten son, begotten, not of nothing, but of the Father, not as a created being, but as one who is begotten." The Council condemns "those who think or say that the Son of God is a creature, or brought into being, or made, and that he is not truly a being who is begotten." The Council of Nicaea in 325 thus defines the faith of the Church in regard to the generation of the Son: "We believe in one God, the Father, almighty, creator of all things visible and invisible, and in one Lord, Jesus Christ, Son of God, only begotten, begotten of the Father, that is, from the substance of the Father, God of God, light of light, true God of true God, begotten, not created, consubstantial with the Father."

We see how by these solemn definitions the Church expresses the distinction which it means to uphold between the generation of the Son and the creation of the world. The Son, who is begotten, comes from the substance of the Father; he is consubstantial with the Father. Created being is not consubstantial with the Father, nor does it come from his substance. The Gnostic systems, up to and including the Hegelian system, always confuse the generation of the Son and the creation of the world.

Athanasius of Alexandria, in his great dispute with the Arians, develops this distinction. According to the Arians, he tells us, the Logos is a creation and a work of God. He is not Son by nature, nor is he of the substance of the Father. He is only Son by grace, as we men, too, are called sons by grace. God was not always Father, and there was a time when God existed alone; he was not yet Father; it was only later that he became Father. Everything has been made out of nothing, and the Logos of God was himself made out of nothing; there was a time when the Logos did not exist; he did not exist before coming into being. He did not exist before being generated. Athanasius replies to the Arians in his great book against the Arians: "If the Logos does not coexist eternally with the Father, then the Trinity is not eternal. In that case God as one alone existed previously, and it is by increase that it finally became threefold." Analysing the passages of Scripture advanced by the Arians, Athanasius shows that the Son is not a creature, but is of the substance of the Father. We must distinguish, Athanasius tells us, between the creative act of God and the act of generation. The act of generation is first; it is coeternal with God. The act of creation is second. The Son is begotten; he is in strict truth from that blessed and eternal divine substance. Created things, on the other hand, are set in being outside God by an act of his will. In regard to creation Moses did not say: "In the beginning God generated . . .", or, "In the beginning was . . .", but, "In the beginning God created . . .". On the other hand, in regard to the Son, Scripture does not say, "I created thee", but, "I have begotten thee" (Ps. 2. 7). When it speaks of creation Scripture expresses itself thus: "In the beginning God created . . .". When it speaks of the generation of the Son Scripture declares: "In the beginning was the Logos." God calls man to be adopted. By grace he becomes Father of men, and they become by grace sons, when they receive in their hearts the Spirit of adoption. But by nature men are created. Since the eternal Son of God is Son by nature, he is begotten.

This distinction between creation and generation is fundamental. The Gnostic and Neoplatonist systems always confuse creation and generation, and make of creation a generation in which created being is regarded as consubstantial with the One, or the divine substance. This is the philosophical tradition which runs from Plotinus to Spinoza and Hegel. According to Christian metaphysics the creature, and in particular the human soul, is not, as we shall see, by nature from the divine substance. It is called to share the life of God, but by grace.

CREATION AND BEGINNING: CREATION IS AN IRREVERSIBLE PROCESS: CRITICISM OF THE MYTH OF THE EVERLASTING RETURN

According to the metaphysical systems of India as expressed, for example, in the Upanishads, according to the

Orphic myth, according to Plato, Aristotle and Plotinus, the world comes eternally, with different modalities, from the divine. According to the Brahmanical theosophy the world is a representation or a dream of the absolute; we are parts of the absolute sunk in the illusion of the many. Our duty is to overcome this illusion, and to return to the One from which we eternally come forth. The world is the place of illusion, of grief and of care. But this coming forth, this illusion, seems eternal and necessary, as was later held by Spinoza and Fichte. According to Plato the world is divine, and it is eternal. According to Aristotle the world is uncreated, imperishable, escaping from the becoming inherent in matter because its substance is divine. According to Plotinus the downward movement which goes from the one to the many is an eternal movement. The world is eternal. The idea of the eternity of the world is an idea common both to Indian and Greek metaphysics.

But the phenomenon produced by becoming presents a problem. If there is change in the world, becoming, generation and corruption, how can this becoming have a place in the eternity of the cosmos? Plato, like Aristotle and like Plotinus, repeats the old myth of the everlasting return. Becoming is cyclic. Socrates will for ever be judged again and again, and will again drink the hemlock. The Trojan war is before us, but it is also after us in a future cycle.

Finally, the human soul is itself part of the divine substance: that is the teaching of Brahmanism, Orphism, Platonism, Neoplatonism and Gnosticism. It is of the divine essence, and hence is uncreated and eternal. It has fallen into a body, into this world of care and grief. The pre-existence of the soul guarantees its immortality. All souls pre-existed in the womb of the one from all eternity. There is no real creation of souls which, as Bergson said, did not in any sense pre-exist. Everything pre-exists. Time, the sign of creation in process of development, is thus illusory. It is illusory, just like space or the many.

Against all these theories and tendencies, deeply embedded in the ancient metaphysical tradition, both Indian and Greek, Christian thought was to react and it expressed itself plainly. According to Christian metaphysics, the principles and roots of which rest in Scripture, the world of the many is not appearance or illusion. Multiplicity of souls is not the result of a fall or failure. Human souls are not parts of the divine substance, but are created, and created as new souls, radically, ontologically, distinct from God their creator. All beings are beginning to be born and to exist. We are in a world which is in a state of coming into being, of continued creation, in which all beings every day begin to exist. According to Scripture, the whole world has had a beginning, and will have an end, for it is not divine, and is not the same as self-existence. God alone is the rock on which we rest.

St Irenaeus refers again to the theory that souls could not be immortal if they had not pre-existed from all eternity. He replies: some people say that souls which began to exist shortly before cannot exist for long in the future: necessarily, either they were not born if they are to be immortal, or if they had a beginning they must die with the body. Those who say this should learn from us that God alone is without beginning and without end, always and truly the same. But all beings that are derived from him, all created beings, had a beginning of their existence. Nevertheless they will continue to exist throughout the ages, by the will of God who created them, and who gives them their birth at the beginning and after that their permanence (*Adv. Haer.*, 2, 34, 2).

We see that the doctrine about time is bound up with cosmology, if properly understood, and also with anthropology and ontology and even theology. A whole theology lies beneath the ancient doctrine of the eternity of the world and the everlasting return: a pantheistic theology.

Origen, who thought indeed that he could adopt some metaphysical theories which were radically opposed to the principles and requirements of Christian metaphysics, nevertheless saw clearly that the doctrine of the everlasting return was itself incompatible with Christianity. In his book against Celsus, Origen criticizes the theory of the Neoplatonist philosopher who wrote: "From beginning to end the course of mortal things is alike, and the same things which have existed must always exist in the present and continue in the future according to fixed cycles" (quoted by Origen, *Contra Celsum*, 4, 65).

If this were true [answers Origen] there would be an end to our freedom. Indeed, if according to periodic cycles the same events must eternally take place among mortals in the past, present and future, it is quite plain that Socrates will necessarily and eternally practise philosophy, and be accused of having introduced new gods and corrupted the youth. Anytos and Melitos will accuse him eternally, and the court will eternally condemn him to die by the hemlock.... If this is so, I do not see how our freedom can be preserved.... If the theory of Celsus is granted, it is thus necessary that eternally, according to fixed periods, Moses must leave Egypt with the Hebrews, Jesus must come into this life to perform the same acts he has already performed, not once only but an infinity of times, from period to period. And it will be the same people who will be Christians in the cycles which return in a fixed order. Celsus will again write this book, which he has already written an infinity of times before (*Contra Celsum*, 4, 67).

In his book *De Principiis* Origen had in the same way refuted the myth of the everlasting return in the name of human freedom:

I do not know by what proofs those can support their assertion who say that there follow one another again and again exactly similar worlds, alike in every respect to one another. If it is said that a second world will be exactly similar to this one, Adam and Eve must do once again what they did in this world; the flood must occur again; Moses must again lead out of Egypt a nation of six hundred thousand men; Judas must betray the Lord a second time; a second time must Paul look after the garments of those who stone Stephen.... I do not think that this theory can be upheld on any reasonable ground, if it is true that souls are brought to act by freedom of choice, if their progress and their falls should be attributed to the power of their own wills. In fact souls are not forced to follow a course of action which, at the end of many centuries, is repeated in the same circle (*De Princ.*, 2, 3, 4–5).

The myth of the everlasting return was to have a long life. We find it referred to in certain theosophical speculations of the twelfth century, then in the thirteenth century in the esoteric Jewish mystical philosophy, called Kabbalah, mentioned by Siger de Brabant; in the sixteenth century in the philosophical schools which sought to revive Neoplatonism; at the end of the nineteenth century in Nietzsche; and at the present day in a number of theosophical sects.

According to Christian metaphysics creation takes place once, and is irreversible. Christ came and died and rose again once only. The irreversible character of creation is the reason, on the ontological level, for the measureless gravity of each of our acts.

Basil of Caesarea, in his *Homilies on the Hexaemeron*, criticizes the notion of an eternity of the world which, in Greek philosophy from Heraclitus and Plato to Aristotle and Plotinus, is bound up with the doctrine of the divinity of the world, with pantheism.

Do not suppose that the visible world had no beginning. Because the stars in their movement through the heavens pass in a circle around us, and because the beginning of the circle escapes the direct perception of our senses, we cannot conclude that there have always existed bodies involved in this circular movement.... Do not let yourself be deceived by the mistaken idea of a world without beginning or end. For, says Scripture, the figure of this world passes away, and heaven and earth will pass away. The doctrines of the consummation of the universe and of the transformation of the world are introduced briefly by the elementary teaching of the inspired doctrine: "In the beginning God created...". That which began in time must necessarily end also with time. If creation has a beginning in time, we cannot doubt about the end (*op. cit.*, 1, 2, 3).

It is, writes Ambrose of Milan, in order to refute the false doctrine of the eternity of the world, conceived as coeternal with God, that holy Scripture starts thus: "In the beginning God created heaven and earth..." (*Hexaemeron*, 1, 2). It is also in order that we may not think that the world is uncreated, sharing in the divine substance. How can the pagans hold that the world is eternal, associate it thus with the Creator of all things, claim for the created equality with the Creator, and suppose that the bodily matter of the world can be joined with the invisible and unapproachable nature of God (*op. cit.*, 1, 3)? It is not in vain that the passage in the Bible teaches us about creation. For many Gentiles, who hold that the world is coeternal with God, like the shadow of divine power, assert too that the world subsists in virtue of its own strength, of itself; though they admit that God is the cause of the world, nevertheless they hold that the world is made not by God's will and decree but in the same way that the body is the cause of its shadow. The shadow clings to the body, and the light to the lamp, rather by natural necessity than by a voluntary and deliberate act (1, 5). It is at the beginning of time that God created heaven and earth. For time exists as long as the world exists; it did not exist before the world (1, 6). When the pagans ask why God waited so long before sending salvation to mankind, Ambrose replies: "The universe, like all things, has had imperfect beginnings, so that the Christian faith, far advanced in years, may set the crown on its venerable age. Those who find fault with this might as well blame the harvest because it is slow to ripen, or the vintage because it comes only at the end of the year, or the olive because its fruit is the last to mature" (*Epist.*, 18, 28). In this passage Ambrose expresses, in a picture, his intuition of the nature of time: time implies that the reality is not achieved all in a moment; it implies a progressive creation, a process of ripening.

To meet the Jewish and Christian doctrine of creation some non-Christian philosophers raised objections which gave Christian philosophers a hard puzzle to solve. Proclus, among many others, formulated as follows one of the fundamental objections against Christians raised by the philosophers who were heirs to Hellenism: "For what reason should God, after doing nothing for infinite time, start to create? Because he thinks it is better? But, previously, either he did not know this, or he knew it. To say that he did not know it is absurd, while, if he did know it, why did he not begin sooner?" (*Commentary on the Timaeus*, 88c).

Christianity introduced, indeed, a new conception of time, and of the relations between time and eternity. According to the biblical and Christian view of the world, time is the measure of that irreversible creation which is still taking place today, and which is hastening to its conclusion. Hence time is not, as Plato thought, a changing image of eternity, nor is it, as Plotinus taught, evidence of a fall. Time is the measure of a creation in process of realization. Before creation there was no time. Before creation there was God, who creates in his eternal present, his eternal noontime. We are created in God's present moment.

St Augustine struggled with these difficult problems. In his first works he rebuts the objection. The opponents of Christianity say: "If God created heaven and earth with a beginning in time, what did he do before he created heaven and earth? Why did he choose suddenly to do what he had never done before throughout everlasting time?" Augustine, in his commentary on Genesis, replies against the Manichees:

God, in the beginning, *in principio,* created heaven and earth. But this beginning is not a beginning in time. This beginning is the Word who was with the Father (*De Gen. contra Manich.,* 1, 3). Like Philo of Alexandria and like Origen, Augustine, in this passage, leaves aside the literal meaning of the biblical text in its Hebrew sense (*bereshit bara*), and allegorizes. The beginning in time of creation becomes a principle outside time, the Logos.

However, already in this early book Augustine adds another explanation. Even if we admit that God created heaven and earth with a beginning in time, we must understand that before the beginning of time there was no time. God created time itself, and so, before he made time, there was no time. Thus we cannot say there had been a time when God had not yet created. If time begins to exist with heaven and earth, we cannot find a time when God had not yet created heaven and earth (*ibid.*). We do not say that the world is coeternal with God, for the eternity of the world is not the same as God's eternity. God created the world, and thus time began to exist together with the creation itself which God made (1, 4).

In the *Confessions* Augustine repeats the same argument:

> Is it not true that those commit their old mistake who ask us, what did God do before he created heaven and earth? (11, 10, 12). How could countless ages have passed, since you who are the cause and author of the ages would not have yet created them? How could there have been time, if you had not yourself made it?... It was you who would have made this time. If, on the other hand, there was no time before heaven and earth existed, why ask what you did "then"? When there was no time, neither was there a "then". No, you did not exist in time, before time existed.... You existed before time by the whole height of your ever-present eternity.... Your present moment is eternity (*Ibid.*, 11, 13).

Again, in *The City of God,* Augustine returns to the problem. "Those who agree, as we do, that God created the world, but who ask us when the world began, should consider carefully what answer they would make to the question: where was the world made? In exactly the same way that we are asked why it was made at this moment and not before, we may ask why it was made where it is and not elsewhere ..." (11, 5). "The world was not created in time, but with time" (11, 6).

In Book XII of *The City of God* Augustine analyses and criticizes the myth of the everlasting return: "Such beliefs are not for us! Once only did Christ die for our sins, and having risen from the dead he dies no more ..." (12, 14).

After St Augustine Christian philosophers, like Aeneas of Gaza, Zacharius of Mitylene, Procopius of Gaza and John Philoponus criticize and reject the Greek doctrines of the everlasting return and the eternity of the cosmos.

It is on the authority of Scripture that the Fathers reject the doctrine of the eternity of the world, and admit the idea of a beginning of creation. Christianity imposes this view of the world upon them. In the thirteenth century the same problems were again debated. The Arab philosophers brought to the Latin West an Aristotle mingled with Neoplatonist comments. The theory of the eternity of the world appears as one of the leading theories of Aristotelianism, identified by some with philosophical reason itself. St Thomas Aquinas rightly distinguished between the idea of creation and the idea of beginning. It is not the same thing to say: the world is created, and to say: it is not everlasting. Strictly speaking, and as a matter of pure reason, we could conceive a world which was everlasting, and yet created. The question whether the world is everlasting or not, says St Thomas, is not within the province of human reason. Pure reason cannot show that the world had a beginning. It is revelation which teaches us this.

Today these problems are looked at in a somewhat different light. St Thomas wrote that it could not be proved that the human race is not everlasting: today we know that the human race had a beginning in time, and that all living things began, that the earth has a definite age, and also the universe. The idea of an everlasting universe can scarcely be accepted any longer, as a result of the outlook produced by modern science. The universe could be conceived as everlasting when the world was looked at as divine, and as escaping from becoming (the universe of Aristotle). Today we know that everything in the universe is in a state of evolution and of birth. What today can perhaps strictly be conceived or imagined as everlasting is not our concrete universe, but creation itself. In other words, instead of the hypothesis of an everlasting universe Christian philosophers can today tackle the hypothesis of a creation everlastingly renewed. The state of the problem has changed.

CHAPTER III

CHRISTIAN

ANTHROPOLOGY

CRITICISM OF PLATONIC ANTHROPOLOGY

The biblical tradition carries with it, as we have seen, a certain doctrine concerning man, a certain anthropology. Man is created. He is not made from the substance of God. He is not a divine soul fallen into an evil body. Man is a living, created soul, in his present bodily state. Man is flesh, not by accident, nor owing to a fall, but by creation.

Indian thought, and the philosophies of ancient Greece, also carried with them certain traditions, certain tendencies, and certain theories with regard to anthropology. In the Brahmanic writings we find plainly taught that the human soul is part of the absolute divine substance, part of the absolute, but separated and exiled in bodies which multiply the one soul in a number of parts or points in view. Wisdom or knowledge consists in recognizing the unity of all beings: all these many souls, all these many beings, only make up one. We are nothing else than the absolute. The practice of asceticism should allow us to reach again the unity we have lost.

This line of thought appears, too, in the Orphic fragments and traditions, then in Empedocles, in Plato, in the early works of Aristotle, in the Hermetic books, in the Gnostic systems and in Plotinus.

Against this anthropology orthodox Christian thought had to formulate its own teaching in harmony with the principles and metaphysical requirements of Christianity.

From the time of Justin we find these theories rejected. In his *Dialogue with Tryphon* the Christian philosopher discusses and rejects the Platonic teaching that the soul is by nature divine, and the myth of the transmigration of souls. The human soul, writes Justin, is not of itself life, but has received life. Thus it is not of itself, by nature, immortal, for life does not belong to it as its own, in the way that it belongs to God (*op. cit.*, 4–6).

It sounds at first paradoxical to say that the Fathers criticized the Platonic teaching about the immortality of the soul. But this paradox is explained if we reflect that the immortality of the soul in Plato's view rests on the fact that the soul is by nature divine and uncreated. Now the Fathers will not admit this metaphysical theory. That is why they reject the idea of an immortality natural to the soul, which in order to gain a happy eternity would only have to return to the home from which it has fallen.

"The human soul is not of itself immortal", wrote Tatian to the Greeks. "It is mortal; but this same soul is also able not to die." It is the gift of God, of the Spirit of God, who gives immortality to the soul, and not its own nature (*Oratio ad Graecos*, 13).

Irenaeus repeats Justin's criticism of the Platonic teaching. The Lord, writes Irenaeus, taught in the clearest fashion that not only does the soul continue in existence after death, and that souls do not pass from one body to another, but also that they keep the "character" of this body, that by which they are adapted to one body and not to another; indeed they remember the actions performed here on earth. The parable of the wicked rich man and the poor man, Lazarus (Luke 16) shows plainly that souls continue to exist, that they do not pass from one body to another, that they possess those human characteristics by which they can be recognized, and that they remember those who are on earth (*Adv. Haer.*, 2, 34, 1).

It is not of ourselves nor of our own nature that we possess life: life is given in accordance with God's grace.... Just as the animal body is not itself the soul, but shares in the soul, so far as God wills, so too the soul itself is not life, but receives from God a share in life. It is God who gives life, and unending existence (2, 34, 2).

In his book devoted to the question of the soul Tertullian criticizes and rejects certain theories central to Platonic anthropology. Plato, writes Tertullian, holds that the soul is unborn and uncreated. We on our part teach that it is born, that it is created, and that it has a beginning (*De anima*, 3, 4).

> Some people think they have come down from heaven, and they are as certain of this belief as of their assurance of returning thither.... I am sorry that Plato with the best intentions spread all these heresies. Indeed from him came the theory, taught in the *Phaedo*, that the souls on earth come from on high, and that they will return on high.... To persuade us of this teaching, and of the belief that the soul first passed its life in heaven with God in the exchange of ideas, and that it has been brought down here from on high, and that it remembers here on earth what it knew formerly of the ideal patterns, Plato worked out a fresh argument, namely, that to learn is to remember: when souls come from on high down to earth, at first they forget the objects of their former contemplation, then, taught by visible objects, they remember them. Since the teaching which the heretics borrow is thenceforth recommended by an argument of this kind, through the influence of Plato, I shall refute the heretics sufficiently if I refute Plato's argument (*op. cit.*, 23, 1–6).

First, argues Tertullian, I shall not grant Plato that the soul can forget, since in other respects Plato allows to the soul a divinity such that it is accounted equal to God. Plato declares that the soul is uncreated, which is enough to establish its full divinity. Plato adds that it is immortal, incorruptible and incorporeal, because he assigns these attributes also to God. What more could he assign to the soul, if he said it was divine? We, who hold that nothing is equal to God, hold for that reason that the soul is far lower than God, because we recognize that the soul is born and created, and hence divine in a far lesser way. Forgetfulness on the part of the soul is conceivable from the Christian point of view. But, on the Platonic hypothesis, forgetfulness on the part of the soul contradicts the doctrine of the soul's divinity. Tertullian analyses and discusses at length Plato's theories concerning the soul, and rejects his teaching about the soul's divinity, pre-existence, and fall, as also of course his teaching about the transmigration of souls from body to body.

Clement of Alexandria is aware of this ancient teaching found in the tradition of Greek thought, and some passages might even let us suppose that he supports it. But other passages formally exclude the teaching: "It is not, then, true, that the soul is sent here below as to a less good destiny..." (*Stromata*, 4, 26, 167). "We could not exist before God made us. For we should need to know where we were, if our pre-existence were admitted, and how and why we have come here below" (*Eclogae propheticae*, fr. 17). In Book III of the *Stromata* Clement discusses and refutes the theories of Marcion, as well as the teaching of the soul's fall, and defends marriage. It will be seen that the Christian teaching about marriage has often been the obstacle preventing orthodoxy from accepting the Platonic myth. Marriage is good, and is a sacrament. The generation of children has a blessing upon it. If the myth of the soul's fall were true, every conception, every birth, would be a disaster, causing a divine soul to fall from heaven, where it was happy, into

an evil body. This contradicts the blessings which the Old
Testament and the New Testament give to marriage. Marriage
cooperates in the work of creation, writes Clement (*op. cit.,*
3, 9, 66). Generation of children obeys the creator's com-
mand, when he said, "increase and multiply". If birth is
evil, then the Lord is involved in evil, seeing that he has
shared in birth, and so, too, the Virgin who brought him
forth. Those who speak against the generation of children
blaspheme the will of God and the mystery of creation (3,
17, 102). How would the purpose of the Church be fulfilled
without the body, since the Lord himself, who is the head
of the Church, came in the flesh? (3, 17). Hence those are
wrong who heap abuse on creation, and decry the body.
Everything comes from one God, creator both of soul and
body (4, 26).

Arnobius, in other respects far from orthodox, criticizes
the Platonic, Gnostic and Neoplatonic myth of the essential
divinity, pre-existence and fall, of the soul: "There is no
danger that we shall be deceived and abused with vain
promises by that which is said by some new arrivals who
raise themselves too high in the opinion they have of themselves, saying that souls are immortal, all near in rank and
dignity to the Lord who is cause of what exists" (*Adversus
nationes*, 2, 15–16). Arnobius, like Tertullian, but with still
greater vehemence, criticizes the reasoning of the philosophers
who claim that the soul of itself is divine, and has fallen
here below into an evil body. If the soul is immortal, this
is not due to its own nature. Addressing these philosophers
Arnobius writes:

> It is in yourselves that you place the salvation of your souls;
> it is by your own efforts alone that you possess the assurance
> of becoming gods. We, on the other hand, promise nothing
> from our weakness, since our nature has no power, and in
> every struggle yields to its passions. . . . You believe that, being
> scarcely freed from the bonds of the flesh, you will have wings

which will enable you to reach heaven and fly up to the stars. We, on the other hand, fear such audacity; we do not think ourselves able to reach the dwellings on high, for we are not even sure that we deserve to receive life and to escape from the laws of mortality. You indeed claim that you will return of yourselves to the court of the Lord as to your own home, with nothing to hinder you. We, for our part, have no hope that this could come about without the help of the Lord of all things, and we do not think it right to attribute to any man such power and such great liberty (2, 33).

We can see that what Arnobius criticizes in an anthropology which attributes divine characteristics to the soul is the self-sufficiency thus given to the soul, a self-sufficiency which approximates to the Pelagian heresy. From the Christian point of view the soul, which is created, only reaches beatitude by the grace of God.

THE ORIGENIST MYTH

Christian thought, as we have seen, from the time of Justin, rejected certain theories which were central to Platonic, Neoplatonic and Gnostic theories. In rejecting these theories Christian anthropology became aware of its own nature. A crisis which was particularly grave and important allowed this awareness of itself to find full expression.

Origen of Alexandria, in a book called *De principiis*, employed some metaphysical theories which were close to those of Plotinus. It will be well to give a brief account of the system which appears in the *De principiis*. Of this we have only a Latin translation which has been touched up, and some Greek fragments, or translations from the Greek, which enable us to reconstruct the original in outline.

At the beginning there is the One, the Monad, the Henad; God is understanding, and the source from which come all intellectual natures or intelligences. God is absolutely one and simple.

God is the creator. In maintaining this basic assertion of Jewish and Christian metaphysics Origen departs from Neo-platonic metaphysics, which set aside the idea of creation in the strict technical sense which it bears in Jewish and Christian thought. Matter is not coeternal with God. This world had a beginning of its existence. Yet, according to Origen, creation is eternal, that is to say, before this world there had been others, and after this world there will still be others. The *bereshit, in principio,* which comes at the beginning of the first chapter of the Bible and of the Gospel of St John, does not imply a beginning in time. The beginning in which all has been created is the Logos of God, the Christ. Creation is eternal. God could not be called almighty had there not existed from all eternity beings upon which he exercises his whole power.

The power of God is limited. The number of rational substances created is not infinite. The power of God is finite, for, if it were infinite, it would not understand itself, since the infinite is by nature incomprehensible. Thus God has created as many beings as he could keep within his attention and his providence.

At the beginning—that is, from all eternity—God creates pure intellectual substances. In point of fact, in view of certain fragments of the *De principiis* which are only preserved in a Latin translation by St Jerome, the question may be asked whether the doctrine of creation has been fully preserved in this connection. For, according to one of these passages, Origen wrote: "All rational natures, that is to say, the Father and the Son and the Holy Ghost, the angels, the powers, the dominations, and the other virtues, man himself in view of the dignity of his soul, are of a single substance...." If created beings are of one substance with God, if they are consubstantial with God, they are not, strictly speaking, created. They are, like the Word, begotten from eternity of God the Father.

So, too, the Emperor Justinian, in a letter addressed to the fathers of the fifth General Council, thus sums up the teaching of the monks of the sixth century, called "Origenists", who were then far removed from the time of their Alexandrian master. "The intellectual substances were beyond all number and all description, so that rational beings made up a unity through identity of substance and of activity.... Having come, so to speak, from an overflow of God's charity and of divine contemplation, they were clothed with finer or with grosser bodies according to the tendency of each for what is worse, and they received names."

This passage cannot, certainly, be applied just as it is to Origen's own teaching, but the connection between this passage and more ancient evidence compels us to ask whether the Origenist monks of the fifth century had not deduced fairly accurately, from the principles laid down by Origen himself, consequences which he himself would perhaps have balanced with others and corrected, though at the cost of the system's logic.

The evidence of Leontius of Byzantium, of Epiphanius and of Jerome enables us to reconstruct the Origenist teaching about the fall as follows:

Before the creation of the world all intellectual substances were sinless; they served God and observed his commandments. But the devil incited the spiritual powers to turn away from God. Some sinned gravely, and became devils; others sinned less gravely, and became angels; others still less gravely, and became archangels; thus each was given a state corresponding to its sin. There remained the souls which had not committed so great a sin as to become devils, nor so small a sin as to become angels. For them God created the present world, and he bound the soul to the body, as a punishment. The variety of beings is thus explained by the variety of degrees of their fall. For God is not unjust. Why, indeed, should some people be born blind or lame, if not on account of previous sin? Pure spiritual substances were thus deprived of their first beatitude, and rendered bodily in different degrees, and separated from one another.

This subject of the fall and of the dispersion of souls is one that is developed at length by Plotinus. The system of Plotinus and the system which seems to have provided the basis for Origen's book, the *De principiis*, have a profound similarity.

The cause of the fall, in systems of this kind, always remains mysterious. For why should spiritual substances, which were happy and enjoyed the contemplation of the one, be separated and fall into this world of misery and care? Origen replies that it is on account of negligence and laziness that pure spiritual natures have fallen. Other passages, as we have seen, speak of surfeit and disgust. The fall, as we have seen, is progressive and gradual.

Spiritual natures are responsible for their fall, for they have been created free. This emphasizes the difference between Origen's system and the Gnostic systems. The devil himself was created good and free. His nature was not evil from eternity, and as created. He was evil by free choice.

"Original sin", in Origen's eyes, is thus a pre-cosmic sin, before the creation of the world, since the world was created to receive sinful souls. This myth clearly has nothing in common with the teaching of the third chapter of Genesis, which speaks of the sin of actual man, and of an historical sin, occurring when the world existed, moreover at a later period, since man was created last. Hence, from this point of view, the Origenist outlook is completely opposed to that of the Bible. According to the Bible God created the world by an act of free will previous to all sin. According to Origen, the material, physical world is the result of the sin of pre-existing souls. According to the Bible, man was created with a body before any sin. According to Origen, the body is the prison created by God to receive sinful souls. According to the Bible, the variety and multiplication of souls is the result of a deliberate creative act and is blessed by God. According to Origen, the variety manifests an unequal fall, different in degree and in gravity.

To be material is thus, according to Origen, a consequence of the fall, but yet it is God who created matter. Matter is not an eternal, uncreated, principle, as in dualism of the Manichaean type. It is not eternal and uncreated, as Aristotle and many Greek philosophers after him supposed. Nor is it that final degradation, that darkness which the light shed by the One cannot enlighten, as with Plotinus. It is not, as with Plotinus, the principle of division and variation. It is the work of God, the creator, who formed a world to receive fallen souls.

Like Plotinus, Origen shares the ideas of his time with regard to cosmic animism. The sun, the moon and the stars, are, in Plotinus's view, divinities. To Origen they are fallen souls, but not very gravely fallen. They have been made subject to the vanity of matter, and await their deliverance. They long to be freed and delivered, so as to be with Christ.

Origen thus employed the ancient Orphic theory of the pre-existence of souls and of their fall into bodies, in which they are, so to speak, imprisoned. Created spirits have become souls because their charity and their zeal has become cold. The Gnostic contrast between *pneuma* and *psyche*, derived through a misinterpretation from certain letters of St Paul, is adapted by Origen to suit his own system. Souls as they actually exist are fallen spirits. Bodies are those garments of skin which God made for Adam and Eve. Before the fall spiritual substances were naked and sinless. Now they are clothed with bodies.

Happily the fall is not final. As with Plato, so with Origen, there is a return movement, a going up again to the One. This movement has the effect of undoing all that the fall has done, or of repairing, from the opposite point of view, all that the fall has damaged. Thus the return will be at first a liberation from the body, a disincarnation, a de-materialization. From this we see, as St Jerome remarks, what Origen can think of the resurrection. Bodily substances will be completely abolished. Souls will rise again towards their principle, towards God, by moving back from the point to which they have fallen. This is the restoration (*apokatastasis*) of all things. The soul will again become spirit.

Since created natures are free, they will be able to begin again eternally this fall and this cycle. Hence God will have eternally to create worlds which can receive them. The present world had indeed a beginning in time, as the Bible teaches. But before this world and after this world God has created and will create other worlds on account of the freedom, and, I may add, the instability of created spiritual natures. Successive worlds are not identical with one another. Origen does not employ the myth of the everlasting return, which, moreover, he criticizes. Nor does he precisely employ the myth of the transmigration of souls from body to body. This myth, too, he criticizes. But he teaches that after a cycle, in which a particular soul has sunk down to a particular degree, it could in another cosmic cycle fall still lower, for example, to the degree of an animal or even a vegetable.

The Origenist myth has had its descendants, a considerable posterity. We find some fairly important traces of it in the work of Evagrius Ponticus (fourth century), among the Origenist monks who provoked the condemnations of the fifth General Council, and also in the twelfth century in the speculations of the Catharists, in the Kabbalist writings of the same period, and, still later, at the beginning of the nineteenth century in the German philosopher Schelling. We also find them in our own time in many theosophical speculations. The Origenist myth gives a confused and incoherent expression to one of the earliest themes of ancient animist and pre-logical human thought.

Orthodox Christian thought, when faced with this myth, had to react with energy. The interest of the struggle thus provoked resides chiefly, I think, in this reaction which was provoked, and which allowed Christian thought to clarify itself in face of such confused speculations. We shall see with what sanity, what sense of objective reality, what balance, orthodoxy has got rid of this Origenist myth. Origen, we must not forget, was an amazing genius. His influence was great. Those who stood up against Origen were not great philosophers; they were often far more ordinary, and indeed mediocre, minds. But orthodoxy in the Church does not necessarily depend on genius. The Church is free in its treatment of its greatest doctors, and more so of its "intellectuals", even the most brilliant. Of the theories of Origen, who was the genius of his time, it has retained but little, and has got rid of much.

CRITICISM OF THE ORIGENIST MYTH

Methodius of Olympus, in a dialogue on the resurrection, criticizes the theories of Origen. "Man is by nature neither soul without body nor body without soul, but a synthesis brought about by union of soul and body in a single form, which is beautiful. Origen, for his part, claimed that the soul alone makes up man, as does Plato . . ." (op. cit.).

From these words we see that from the first centuries orthodox Christian thought had become aware of certain requirements in questions of anthropology, and we see that these requirements were already formulated in a way that prefigures the formulas of St Thomas Aquinas. Before Methodius, Irenaeus had already written: "Since man is a living being, composed of body and soul, it is right and necessary to take account of these elements" (Proof of the Apostolic Preaching). Christian anthropology, for fundamental reasons arising from its very nature, could not be dualist, since the Creator is one, and man, by his creation, is made a bodily being. This characteristic is not an accident, arising from a mythical fall.

Methodius of Olympus continues his critical analysis of Origen. Contrary to what Origen says, the body is not a prison for the soul, and souls are not prisoners. The body is not there to form an obstacle to the soul's activities, but rather cooperates with the soul, and acts with it. The garments of skin with which Genesis tells us God clothed man and woman are not bodies (*ibid.*). If the soul fell into a body on account of sins committed before this fall, was not the body then responsible for the evil done by the soul? If the body is given to the soul as a punishment, like a prison, is this for its good or for its harm? The latter suggestion is absurd. No doctor or schoolmaster gives a medicine or a punishment which makes the evil worse. If it is for its good, why does the Platonic tradition make the body responsible for the evil which the soul does in the body? (*ibid.*).

Cyril of Jerusalem confronts the Gnostic dualism with the principle of Christian metaphysics and anthropology: "The God who creates souls and bodies is one" (*Catecheses,* 4, 4). "It is the same God who is both demiurge of souls and of bodies" (4, 18). This latter assertion is not in truth an argument against Origen, who did not deny that God created bodies, but against the Gnostics. The following assertion, on the other hand, is also an argument against Origen: "Know this, too: before being born into this world the soul did not sin at all. But, coming without sin, now we sin through our freedom" (4, 19). Another passage is aimed in general against Platonism and Neoplatonism: "Do not tell me that our body is responsible for sin. . . . The body does not sin by itself, but the soul sins by the body" (4, 23).

Gregory of Nyssa, who owes much to Origen, employs in part the Origenist system and legend, that cyclic system which we have seen appearing in Origen's book: the end is the same as the beginning. If our future state is to be like angels, this is because our first state was like angels:

> The grace of the resurrection is prescribed to us in no other way than as the re-establishment in their first state of those who have fallen. The grace which we await is indeed the return to our former life, when he who has been driven out will be brought back again into paradise. If our life, being once more re-established as it should be, becomes like that of the angels, this is because our life before we sinned was in some sense angelic. Our return to our former state also renders us like the angels (*The Creation of Man*, 17).

According to Gregory of Nyssa, God has given sex to human nature because he foresaw the sin that was to come. In the original plan, had there been no sin, mankind was to be multiplied like the angels by an intellectual act. Sex is thus a sign of our fall, and the difference between man and woman is, so to speak, an anticipated consequence of original sin. This theory was explicitly rejected by St Thomas Aquinas in the article devoted by him to man's condition before original sin (*Summa Theol.*, 1, Qu. 98, art. 3).

In spite of these tendencies, and, as I may say, these *habitus* which characterize his view of the world, Gregory of Nyssa, nevertheless, criticized his beloved master, Origen, in regard to the myth of the pre-existence of the soul and of its fall:

> Some of our predecessors, who wrote the book *De principiis*, taught that souls pre-exist and form, so to speak, a people in a city apart.... Another group of authors [he refers undoubtedly to Methodius of Olympus] keep to the account given by Moses in his description of the fashioning of mankind, and affirm that the soul was created after the body in time.... Both theories must be criticized.... Those who hold the first and maintain that the society formed by souls is older than their existence in the flesh do not seem to me to have freed themselves from the teaching invented by the Greeks about metempsychosis (*The Creation of Man*, 28).

Gregory of Nyssa criticizes this theory at length, and also the teaching about the transmigration of souls which he considers connected with it: "Since man is one, in the composition of his soul and body, his being can only have a single common origin.... Thus it is true that neither does the soul exist before the body, nor the body apart from the soul, but that there is only a single origin for both of them" (*op. cit.*, 29).

In the dialogue with his sister Macrina on the soul and the resurrection, Gregory of Nyssa mentions the same problems and criticizes Origen in the same way. In his life of Moses he criticizes the myth of the transmigration of souls: "The philosophy of other nations also teaches that the soul is immortal: that is one of its welcome and godly fruits. But it teaches also that souls go from one body to another.... That is due to its uncircumcised flesh ..." (2, 40).

Epiphanius, in his *Panarion* against all heresies, blames Origen for these errors: "He says, indeed, that the human soul pre-exists, and that the souls are angels and higher powers, fallen into sin and as a result imprisoned in the body, that they have been sent by God to undergo punishment, in order to receive a first judgement. That is why, he says, the body is called *demas,* because the soul is bound (*dedesthai*) by the body. Origen has employed the old Greek myth" (*op. cit., Heresy* 64). Epiphanius criticizes the exegesis of Origen, by which Origen claims to derive his own teaching from passages of Scripture. In a letter written to John of Jerusalem, preserved for us in a Latin translation by St Jerome, Epiphanius makes the same complaint against Origen:

Can we tolerate any longer these suggestions of Origen— that the souls of men were angels in heaven, that after having sinned on high they were cast down into this world, that being confined in these human bodies as in tombs or sepulchres they pay in them the penalty for their former sins? Are the bodies of the faithful, then, not the temples of Christ but

prisons for the damned?.... If that is true, what becomes
of our faith, and of our preaching of the resurrection?...
and of that well-known blessing addressed to Adam and his
descendants: Increase and multiply; fill the earth? This would
no longer be a blessing, but, according to Origen, a curse,
since he changes angels into souls, and degrades them from
the sublime height of angelic dignity to a lower rank, as though
God could not grant the human race souls as a blessing, unless
the angels fell into sin; so that there would be just as many
failures in heaven as births on earth.... Origen perverts the
meaning of holy Scripture, which is surely different. So also do
Manichees, Gnostics, Ebionites, Marcionites, and other hereti-
cal sects (op. cit., in *Letters of St Jerome*, 51, 4).

Theophilus of Alexandria in his Easter letter of 401, which
has also been preserved for us by St Jerome, shows that
the system of Origen contradicts the Christian doctrine of
creation:

We have not agreed to this teaching: it is on account of the
fall of rational creatures that he supposes bodies have been
formed.... We refuse to think that the soul of the Saviour
was submitted to the same absurdity. We do not admit that the
sun, the moon, the stars in their courses, as well as the wonderful harmony of the universe, that these were the result of
previous causes, that is, of various sins and faults committed
by souls, nor that the goodness of God has been held back
for long, because he could not create visible creatures, if
invisible creatures did not fail. Nor do we call bodily substance "vanity" (as Origen thinks right to do, thus, though
using different terms, coming near to the opinion of Mani)....
He also condemns marriage that is honourable, when he denies
that bodies could not exist unless souls had previously sinned
in heaven, and, being cast down, were confined, so to speak,
in the prison house of the body. Let him think what he likes,
and say it boldly, but let his ears hear us cry out with St Paul:
"marriage is honourable", and "the marriage bed is without
stain". How could it be without stain, if the soul could only
be clothed with flesh after being stained with sin? Anna, the

wife of Elcana, would have been wrong to ask for a man child, since, in order to satisfy the desire of a mere woman, souls in heaven would have been in danger, and one of them, weighed down with sin, would have had to fall to earth and leave its first happiness. When Moses in his prayer said, "May the Lord your God multiply you . . .", what did he ask for? That legions of souls in heaven should commit sin in order to found the people of Israel! It is manifestly sheer contradiction that Moses should ask that the children of Israel shall be multiplied, if he knew that this multiplication was at the price of the ruin of as many souls. . . . If souls, after having sinned, are sent on earth to be born in the body, it was not reasonable that Adam and Eve should be blessed. . . . We thus reach the conclusion that it is not on account of the sins of souls that the nature of the body is determined.

Theophilus of Alexandria thus criticizes the Origenist myth on the basis of the biblical doctrine of creation, of marriage and of the body. But in his Easter letter of 402 it is on the basis of the Christian doctrine of the resurrection that he opposes the myth of the fall of souls:

Origen, then, is unaware that Christ came, not to set free, after the resurrection, souls from bodies, nor to clothe again with new bodies the souls thus freed, making them come down from the heavenly regions, and then clothing them with blood and flesh, but indeed to give the risen bodies incorruption and eternity. Just as Christ, having died, dies no more, and is not conquered by death, so bodies, when they rise after the resurrection, will not have to perish a second time, or more than twice. Death will not hold them under its dominion any longer, and they will not again be reduced to nothing, for it is man as a whole that the coming of Christ has saved.

In the same Easter letter Theophilus criticizes the Origenist teaching according to which God's power is limited: "God's power is not limited to the number of rational creatures he has made."

St Jerome, after being led astray by Origen, criticizes him severely in various letters and books. Jerome makes his own

the criticism of Epiphanius and of Theophilus of Alexandria.
In a book addressed to Pammachius, and aimed at John of
Jerusalem, Jerome, following Epiphanius, recounts the chief
errors contained in Origen's book *De principiis*: his teaching
on the pre-existence and the fall of souls, his denial of the
resurrection of the body, and so on. According to Jerome,
who appears faithful in this to the biblical standpoint, souls
are created at conception. Hence there is no pre-existence
of the soul before the body. There is continued creation of
souls every day at every conception. Jerome relies on the
words in the fourth Gospel: "My Father worketh until now,
and I work." St Augustine was to see difficulties in this
theory on account of its implications with regard to original
sin. If fresh souls are created every day, at every conception,
how are we to suppose that Adam's sin was transmitted?

Did Augustine have direct knowledge of the book of
Origen which was attacked, or did he only have indirect
knowledge? M. Pierre Courcelle, in his distinguished book
Les Lettres grecques en Occident, has dealt with this question,
which we need not consider here. However it may be,
Augustine criticizes and firmly rejects Origen's theories, on
the ground of the biblical and Christian metaphysic of
creation. "It is better to think, as we do, that God was not
brought to create the world by the sins of spirits possessed
of understanding, but that the world was created by God's
goodness" (*Ad Orosium contra Priscillianistas et Origenistas*,
9). In *The City of God* (Book XII) Augustine returns to his
criticism of Origen:

But this is still more astonishing: some who believe with us
that the principle of all things is one, and that no nature,
which is not that which God is, can exist except through this
Creator, have refused to believe that God, who is good, has
created good things.... But they say that souls—which are
not indeed parts of God, but created by God—have sinned by
separating from their Creator. In different degrees, in accord-

ance with their different sins, from heaven to earth, they have, it is said, deserved different bodies, which are, as it were, bonds. That is what the world is; there we have the cause of creation: not the building up of good, but the repression of evil. For this Origen is rightly judged guilty. For, in the book he has called *Peri Archon*, that is, about principles, this is what he thinks, this is what he writes. And I am astonished more than I can say that a man so learned and so versed in Christian literature has not recognized that this teaching is contrary to the meaning of Scripture, which, after every work of God, adds: "And God saw all that he had done, and behold it was very good." Scripture has thus wished us to understand that there is no other cause for the creation of the world than that good things should be brought into being by God who is good. It is a creation in which, if no one had sinned, the world would have been adorned and filled only with things naturally good.

Moreover, in *The City of God* Augustine also criticizes and rejects a certain number of basic theories of the Platonic and Neoplatonic anthropology: pre-existence of the soul, transmigration of souls, everlasting return, and so on. Against the teaching of the transmigration of souls from body to body Augustine opposes the Christian doctrine of the resurrection (*op. cit.*, 10, 30–1). As we know, students of St Augustine dispute about his Neoplatonism. Here we may note in passing that Augustine rejects the fundamental metaphysical theories of Neoplatonism. His "Neoplatonism" therefore, can only be a more or less superficial veneer which does not reach the metaphysical principles which lie at the basis of Christianity.

Cyril of Alexandria criticizes Origen in his commentary on the Gospel of St John, of which considerable portions have been translated and analysed by Dom Diepen in his book *Aux origines de l'anthropologie de saint Cyrille d'Alexandrie*:

If the soul sinned in a previous existence, and if, for this reason, it has been bound to flesh and blood as a punishment,

how does it come about that those who believe in Christ, and
have received forgiveness of their sins, do not at once leave
their bodies, getting rid of the garment given them as a punishment? How can forgiveness of sins be fully granted to man's
soul, so long as it remains in its state of punishment? Yet, very
far from wishing to get rid of their bodies, we see the faithful
add to their profession of faith in Christ profession of the
resurrection of the body. How, then, can we regard as a
punishment that which is here, in the very confession of
faith, an object of veneration? If souls become incarnate on
account of their former sins, and if the nature of the body has
been devised as a state of punishment, how have we profited
from the Lord's victory over death? Has it not rather been
corruption which has helped us by destroying that which
punished us, and by putting an end to the wrath of God? And,
again, should we not have to say that it is reasonable to give
thanks to death rather than to him who has imposed an everlasting punishment by our resurrection from the dead? Yet,
on the contrary, it is surely for having escaped death that we
give thanks. Hence our taking flesh is not a state of punishment
for the soul.

Theodoret of Cyrrhus, in his *Healing of the Heathen Ail-
ments*, mentions the Platonic theory of the pre-existence of
souls: "Pythagoras and Plato describe a crowd of souls without bodies, and say that those who have fallen into any
fault are put into bodies as a punishment. ..." Theodoret,
like the others, analyses and discusses this theory, in the
end rejecting it (*op. cit.*, 5, 13–4).

In the sixth century the Origenist theories, still fully alive
among some Palestinian monks, were condemned by declara-
tions proposed by the Emperor Justinian, and employed, it
seems, by the fifth General Council which met at Constantinople. For the history of Origenism and these condemnations the reader may be referred to the article "Ori-
génisme" in the *Dictionnaire de Théologie Catholique*. Here
I need only mention some passages which are important

from the metaphysical standpoint. Among the fifteen anathemas of the Council of Constantinople we read:

> If anyone accepts the mythical doctrine of the pre-existence of souls, and of the unthinkable re-establishment (in the former state) which is involved in the doctrine, let him be anathema. If anyone says: creation of all rational beings has been creation of intellectual, incorporeal, and immaterial substances, beyond number and name, so that they have all formed a unity by identity of substance, power and activity, and by union with God the Logos, and by knowledge; but that they have been overcome by weariness of divine contemplation, and have turned to what is worse, each in accordance with its inclination for it; that they have taken bodies more subtle or more gross ... let him be anathema. If anyone says: the sun, the moon, the stars, which also formed part of that same unity of rational beings, because they turned aside and inclined towards what is worse, for this reason have become what they are, let him be anathema. If anyone says: rational beings, their divine charity growing cold, have been clothed with grosser bodies, as are ours, and have been called men; that those which have reached the depth of evil have been clothed with bodies that are cold and dark, are, and have been called devils or spirits of evil, let him be anathema.

The reader interested in these condemnations will find a translation of them in my book, already mentioned, on the metaphysics of Christianity. The few anathemas which I have quoted here will be enough, I think, to show how in certain cases the Church takes up positions which are strictly metaphysical, and rejects theories which are strictly metaphysical, thereby adopting contrary theories which are suitable. This has frequently happened. The condemnations of the Priscillianist theories are also metaphysical in character. When, at the Council of Trent, the Church defined its idea of justification, it took up a position on the question of human nature, human freedom and man's capacity to cooperate with God's grace. When, at the first Vatican Council, the Church took up a position on the question of our natural knowledge of God, it defined propositions concerning epistemology which are strictly metaphysical.

As to anthropology, the Church has rejected formally and on several occasions the basic theories of Platonism and of Neoplatonism. According to orthodox Christian thought, the human soul is created, and is not of the divine substance; it does not exist before coming into the body. The body is not a prison for the soul; soul and body are created together. St Thomas, employing the principles of Aristotelian anthropology against a Platonic tradition, picked up the thread of an anthropology which was not dualist, true to biblical anthropology. This is not without importance from the theological point of view. For, if man was a soul fallen into an evil body, we should no longer understand the biblical and Christian doctrine of creation, according to which creation is the work of God's charity, the expression of his splendour, beauty and goodness. We should no longer understand the Incarnation. How could the Logos of God consent to come into an evil matter, a body impure by nature? From a dualist standpoint the Incarnation inevitably appears as a separation from God in an evil world. This is not the Christian idea of the Incarnation. Again, according to the orthodox idea of the Incarnation, the Logos did not come to assume only the human *body* but complete human nature, body and soul, sensibility, thought, will and freedom. Thus the Incarnation is not the same as what the Neoplatonists called *ensomatosis*, descent into bodies. The Incarnation is the union, without confusion of natures, of divine nature and human nature, freely made godlike. Christian theology is not compatible with every form of anthropology. Orthodox Christian theology only becomes aware gradually of its own needs in regard to anthropology, but, as we have seen, in the sixth century Christian theology rejected, as incompatible with its own principles, certain theories which were those of Platonism and Neoplatonism, as well as of Gnosticism.

THE ANTI-MANICHAEAN STRUGGLE

The anti-Origenist struggle had been full of instruction in the sphere of philosophy for Christian thought. The struggle against the Manichees was to be no less instructive. It allowed Christian thought to clarify certain metaphysical propositions which were fundamental to it, while rejecting certain theories which are also incompatible with essential Christianity.

From the end of the third century we can follow the reaction of orthodox Christian thought to the Manichaean heresy. The author of the acts of Archelaus in the fourth century, St Ephrem, and Cyril of Jerusalem dispute with the Manichees. Serapion of Thmuis, in his books against the Manichees, already formulates one of the basic beliefs of Christianity in regard to the problem of evil: evil is not a substance or a hypostasis. It is an action, *praxis*, rather than a substance, and an action which comes from a deliberate choice on the part of those whose free will is evil. It is no more possible to suppose the existence of a soul in itself and substantially evil, born evil, than of a body in itself and substantially evil. What, then, moves the Manichees to make their accusations against the body?

Titus, bishop of Bostra, published four books against the Manichees. The original Greek text has only been preserved in part, and in a defective form, but a Syriac version restores to us the whole work. Mani, writes Titus of Bostra, wished to show that God is not responsible for evil. He supposed God to be confronted with an evil, pre-existing, unbegotten and hostile to God, who is also unbegotten, a living evil against a living God, and ever at war with God. The Manichees did not understand the reason for creation. They abused creation. They formed in their imagination a picture of two substances opposed in their being, mingled together. Whence, they asked, could evil come, if not from a principle of evil? They spoke against all the works of God, and calumniated his most wise government of creation.

Titus of Bostra criticized the Manichaean myth as unreasonable in the name of common sense and of Scripture. How could natural reason admit the idea of two substantially opposed substances, when the term, substance, is assumed as common to them both? Two principles, derived from nothing else, cannot be absolutely opposed. That which is contrary to being is not being. Two *beings* cannot be absolutely contrary to one another, for at least they have being in common, and all the more so two beings underived and coeternal. Mani claims that God wishes to gather to himself the power which he calls soul, and which is exiled in matter. Does that mean that God has suffered a defeat? Sinful souls which are punished are indeed, according to the Manichaean system, parts of the divine soul, separated from it in matter. Could God, then, punish his own nature? It amounts to this, according to Manichaeism: God is passible, while the principle of evil is itself impassible.

In his second book against the Manichees Titus of Bostra asserts the excellence of creation. The Manichees are always asking: whence comes evil? We say nothing else than this: one God has created all things. Hence there is no being which is substantially, by its nature, evil, but everything is good and beautiful. Evil does not come as a result of creation. It is the injustice of sinful man that causes evil, and this evil is not derived from a matter conceived as having no beginning. Man has been created with the power to do good and evil. If man did evil because he could not prevent himself from so doing, God's judgement on man would be unjust. God created man, soul and body. He created him free. If God had not given man this power to act freely, it would have been because God was jealous, depriving man of his freedom, so that man could not become good by free, voluntary, choice. For gold, which is beautiful by nature, is not beautiful by reason or by virtue. Man, on the other hand, is called to be good by virtue and by choice.

The Manichees condemn the procreation of children. They are enemies of the natural order, and wish to stop the course of nature. God has put in man the natural desire for sexual union to draw men to the work of procreation. Bodily pleasure is without blame, if it follows the order and the law of the creator. The same is true of the pleasure of eating and drinking, which is also natural, if it follows the order and measure of creation.

Didymus of Alexandria, in his book against the Manichees, also refutes the teaching of the two principles. Two underived and eternal principles cannot be opposed absolutely and entirely, as the Manichaean teaching claims. For at least they have existence in common. Nothing is evil substantially, for evil is not a substance but a quality. The devil is an angel who was created good by God; if he has become a devil, it is through his own free act.

Epiphanius, in his *Panarion* against all the heresies, employs the criticism of his predecessors against the Manichaean heresy (*Heresy* 66).

It is, however, especially with St Augustine that the struggle against the Manichees becomes broader, deeper and more instructive in the field of metaphysics, as well as in that of theology. Augustine had passed nine years of his life in the Manichaean sect. Thus it is personal experience which he describes in his *Confessions*, and he knows Manichaeism from inside.

In the works of St Augustine the struggle with the Manichees holds a place of great importance. We are given the opportunity, in particular, of reading the record of discussions between Augustine and some leading Manichees,

Fortunatus (in 392) and Felix (in 404). These discussions are most lively and interesting. In the discussion with Fortunatus we watch Augustine striking directly at the principle of the Manichaean heresy:

First of all [says Augustine] I think it is a mistake to suppose that almighty God could suffer violence in a part of himself, and be defiled. ... You say, indeed, that some people or other has rebelled out of the darkness against God's Kingdom; almighty God, when he saw what ruin and devastation threatened his Kingdom, did not offer any resistance to the hostile people, but sent that Virtue which, mingling with evil and with the people of darkness, has constituted that of which the world has been made. Hence it comes about that souls suffer here below, are slaves, err, and are corrupted, so that they have need, as a necessity for them, of a saviour to cleanse them from error, to save them from this indeterminacy, and from slavery. I think it wicked to believe that almighty God has feared an enemy people, and has been subject to the need to plunge us into these troubles (*op. cit.*, 1).

Further on the discussion turns on the nature of the soul. Augustine expresses the orthodox doctrine of the Christian Church against his Manichaean adversary: "I have denied that the soul was of God's substance, by which I mean that I deny that it is God. But yet I think that it comes from God, who is its cause, for it has been created by God" (1, 12). Then the discussion shifts, and turns to the problem of evil and to freedom (1, 17). At the beginning of the second day's discussion Augustine returns to the problem of freedom:

If, then, it is clear that sin only takes place when there is freedom of choice, I want to hear your answer to the question: What evil has been done by the soul, which you call part, or virtue, or word, or such like, of God, that it should be punished by God in order that it should do penance ... when it has itself committed no sin? (2, 20). If the soul is compelled to do evil, it does not itself do the evil. If it is the people of darkness which has sinned, is it not absurd that I should be the person to do penance? (2, 21).

In his discussion with Felix, Augustine again attacks the Manichaean myth in his introductory remarks: if God is almighty, how has the people of darkness been able to approach him? On the other hand, in the Manichaean system there could not be sin in the strict sense. The people of darkness does not sin; it acts according to its nature. Nor does the nature, which is of the light and is good, sin, for it is compelled to act as it does. There must be free will, if there is to be sin. In short, Augustine argues, explaining here his own view, the human soul is subject to the law of evil on account of Adam's sin (2, 8). Further on Augustine attacks Manichaeism for its teaching about redemption. Christ, says Augustine, did not come to set free a part of God which was imprisoned in matter; he did not come to set free the nature of God which had become estranged, as the Manichaean myth teaches. Christ came to set free a creation fallen into sin through its own fault. What God has begotten of himself is quite different from what he has created. The soul has been created by God, and not begotten of the substance of God (2, 17).

In connection with this struggle against Manichaeism we find once again the distinction which we have already noticed as made against Arianism, that between creation and generation. Christian orthodoxy maintained against Arianism that there is a difference between creation and generation: the Logos is begotten of the substance of God, is coeternal and consubstantial with God; it is not created. Here, from the other point of view, Augustine makes the same distinction. The soul is created, it is not consubstantial with God, it is not drawn from God's substance. The confusion between creation and generation appears in the history of philosophy, especially in Hegel, who confuses the generation of the Word and the creation of the world, and who, further, identifies this creation with a separation just as does the Manichaean myth, the difference being that Hegel rejects dualism, the separation from God consisting in a process of self-generation, an evolutionary and tragic process whereby the absolute generates itself and becomes self-conscious, becomes in truth the absolute spirit.

In his book *De Genesi contra Manichaeos* Augustine again attacks Manichaeism, directing his critical analysis at the heart of the myth. What is being questioned by Manichaeism, writes Augustine, is the very essence of God. According to the Manichees, it is the nature of God which is separated, exiled and plunged in misery, since the soul is consubstantial with God, a part of God. On our side we deny this, and say that it is the nature which God has created out of nothing which is in a state of misery, and that, if it has fallen into misery and misfortune, this is not because it has been compelled to do so, but through its own free will. The Manichees say that there exists an evil nature, to which God has been forced to hand over a part of his own substance to be crucified by it. We say, on the contrary, that there is no natural evil, but that all natures are good; all are good, so far as they exist, for God has made all things very good (*op. cit.*, 2, 29, 43). The human soul is created by God, and is thus not a part of God (*ibid.*, 2, 8, 11).

Augustine sets in opposition to Manichaeism the two fundamental principles of Christian metaphysics: 1. God has created all things; 2. Everything that God has created is very good. Evil things are not evil by nature. Sin is the result of human freedom; it is man's work (*De Gen. ad litt. imperf. liber*, 1, 2, 3). "Often, and indeed nearly always, you, Manichees, ask those whom you try to win over to your heresy, whence comes evil.... You ask whence comes evil, and I, for my part, ask you what is evil" (*De moribus ecclesiae cathol. et de moribus Manichaeorum*, 2, 2, 2, 3). "When, then, it is taught in the Catholic Church that God is the author of all natures and of all substances, it is implied at the same time that God is not the author of evil." What, then, is evil? That which destroys, annihilates, corrupts, created nature. Evil is a corruption, and not a nature. Now corruption does not exist of itself, but in the substance which it corrupts, for the substance is not corruption itself. Thus, the thing which is corrupted by corruption is not corruption, is not evil itself. . . . That is why the people of darkness, the race of darkness, of which you speak, if it lacked all good, as you say, could not ever be corrupted; it would have nothing that corruption could deprive it of (*ibid.*, 2, 5, 7).

In his book *Contra epistolam Manichaei quam vocant fundamenti*, Augustine explains that evil, which is corruption, does not come from the creator of natures, but comes from the fact that these natures are created out of nothing. So far as these natures exist, so far as they are, it is God who has made them; but God has not created them so far as they are corruptible. It is from the nothing out of which they are drawn that there comes this capacity for corruption (*op. cit.*, 44).

Manichaeism blamed a pre-cosmic disaster as the cause responsible for the evil in the world. It is an evil nature which had attacked the God of light, and had provoked this conflict, this war, in which parts of God were found to be prisoners, separated, exiled. The present world is made up of two principles in conjunction, the good and the evil principle. Thus evil comes from the evil principle, which is in matter and in our body. "Up to that time", writes Augustine in his *Confessions*, "I thought it was not we who sin, but some other nature which sins in us; and it appealed to my pride to be apart from sin, and, when I did wrong, not to recognize myself as deserving blame before you, O my God, so as to win from you the healing of my soul, and I loved to excuse myself by accusing some other than me that was in me, without being me . . ." (*op. cit.*, 5, 10, 18).

It is the body, according to Manichaeism, and matter which are responsible for the sin which I commit. It is not I myself. Here we notice the character of moral mystification which the Manichaean myth conceals, ever reviving from century to century up to the present day in a more or less hidden and self-conscious way.

Against the Manichaean myth Augustine set up his own conception, his own theory, of evil, and his own system to explain it. The Augustinian theory of original sin was constructed in answer, partly, to the Manichees, and, partly, to the Pelagians. "The Manichees", writes Augustine, "attribute the origin of sin not to free choice, but to the substance of a hostile people. . . . In their view, fleshly concupiscence, by which the flesh lusts against the spirit, is not a weakness found in us as a result of the nature which has been corrupted in the first man . . ." (*De Haeresibus*, 46). We must always bear in mind, when we study the Augustinian theory of original sin, against what background, in what intellectual and psychological context, it was built up. Against the Manichees Augustine wished to find an explanation of evil, pain, death and concupiscence. The Manichees explained evil by a substance which was uncreated and coeternal with God. Augustine rightly rejected this mythical dualism of principles, and suggested two lines of solution: on the one hand corruption comes from the fact that natures are not generated from the substance of God, but created out of nothing (*Contra Epist. Fundam.*, 41); on the other hand, human nature has deserved, in Adam, the punishment of a sin which we have all committed in Adam (*ibid.*, 43).

The Catholic Church, as we know, has not accepted the Augustinian theory of original sin just as it stands; on the contrary, it has modified it a great deal. If we compare the Augustinian teaching on original sin with the Thomist teaching, for example, we appreciate all the progress achieved in this subject (cf. on this question J.-B. Kors, *Le justice primi-*

tive et le péché originel d'après saint Thomas, Kain, Belgium, 1922; the first chapter is devoted to the Augustinian teaching on original sin).

Augustine had, as a result of his time spent as a Manichee, preserved a conception of sex which was not entirely free from certain vague notions, and a sense of guilt, a basic culpability, which we find expressed in his theory of original sin. Or perhaps, on the other hand, Augustine had been drawn into the Manichaean sect by a certain psychology, a certain disposition, in which conflicts with regard to sex had not been overcome. The Manichaean myth is the type of myth dealt with by depth-psychology and analytic psychotherapy.

After Augustine the struggle against Manichaeism continued in the Church from century to century. A book of Evodius, called *De fide contra Manichaeos,* criticizes the Manichaean myth for its conceptions of the two principles, of creation, of evil, of sin and of redemption. Reference may be made, for details about this book, to the pages dealing with the subject in my work mentioned above (pp. 549–53).

Leo the Great, in his *Epistola XV,* describes and condemns the teaching of the Priscillianists. From the metaphysical standpoint the Priscillianist theories are closely related to those of the Manichees, and, in some respects, to those of the Origenists. The Priscillianists, writes Leo the Great, declare that the human soul is of the divine substance, and that the nature of our soul does not differ from the nature of the creator. This impious doctrine, taught by certain philosophers and by the Manichees, is condemned by the Catholic faith, which is aware that no creature, however high and excellent it may be, is of divine nature. The Priscillianists say, moreover, that the devil was never good, and that his nature is not God's work, but that he came forth from chaos and darkness, for he has no creator, but is himself the principle and substance of evil. The Catholic faith, on the other hand, recognizes that the substance of all creatures, spiritual and bodily, is good, and that there is no nature of evil. For it is God who is the creator of all things, and he has made nothing that is not good. Hence it follows that the devil also would be good, if he had remained in the state in which he had been created. The Priscillianists teach, also, that the creation of bodies is the work of the devil. They teach that souls placed in human bodies have existed without bodies, and have sinned in a heavenly dwelling, and that, on account of this sin, may have been cast down from on high. The Catholic faith rejects this doctrine, and teaches, constantly and truly, that the souls of men, before being put into their bodies, did not exist, and that they are set in bodies by none other than God, who is creator both of souls and bodies.

In certain passages of Pseudo-Denys we also find, in the sixth century, expression given to a reaction of orthodoxy against the Manichaean theories. So, too, the struggle with Manichaeism continued in the writing of John Philoponus, Severus of Antioch, and Timotheus of Constantinople (see references given in *La métaphysique du Christianisme*, pp. 555 *et seq.*). After those of St Augustine, we have the records of discussions, whether real or imaginary, between Christians and Manichees. Thus, in the reign of Justinian, a certain Photius, a Manichee, engaged in controversy with a certain Paul, an orthodox Christian (cf. my analysis, *op. cit.*, p. 561). In the eighth century John Damascene, in his *De fide orthodoxa*, criticizes once again the Manichaean dualism and, among the works of John Damascene, a dialogue, attributed to him, describes a discussion between an orthodox Christian and a Manichee (cf. an analysis of this dialogue in my book mentioned above, p. 563). In an appendix to the works of John Damascene, the Greek Patrology gives us a "discussion between John the orthodox and a Manichee", which is also full of life and interest (cf. my analysis, *op. cit.*, pp. 565-6).

In 400 the Council of Toledo reaffirmed the Catholic rule of faith against all heresies, but especially against the Priscillianists.

> We believe in one true God, Father, Son and Holy Ghost, who has made things visible and invisible.... We say that the soul of man is not God's substance nor part of God, but a creature.... [Several anathemas follow:] If anyone says or believes that this world has not been made by almighty God ... let him be anathema. If anyone says or believes that the world has been made by another God, and not by him of whom it is said: in the beginning God created heaven and earth, let him be anathema. If anyone says or believes that the human soul is a part of God, or that it is God's substance, let him be anathema.

At the beginning of the sixth century a Manichee, Prosper, abjured Manichaean teaching. The formula of abjuration, which has been preserved for us, is full of interest from the philosophical point of view. I have translated part of it (*op. cit.*, pp. 568–71). In the sixth century was composed the first Greek formula of abjuration (cf. *ibid.*, pp. 571–2).

The second Council of Braga, in 561, pronounced seventeen anathemas against the Priscillianists, some of which are concerned with metaphysics, and are aimed at dualism in general, at the doctrine of pre-existence and that of the fall of souls (cf. *ibid.* pp. 572–4).

In the ninth century the great Greek formula of abjuration aimed at the Paulicians deals with typically Manichaean theories (cf. my translation, *op. cit.*, pp. 574–6).

In the twelfth century the struggle against the dualist heresy flared up, and the Church declared afresh its own teaching in face of the revival of heresies of the Manichaean type.

This struggle against the Manichaean myth was to be extremely fruitful for Christian thought, for it permitted Christianity to become explicitly aware, so as to formulate them, of certain basic metaphysical propositions, with regard to the absolute and its relations with the world, with regard to matter, the human soul, the human body, evil and freedom. In the struggle with Manichaeism, Christian thought was to formulate some of its most important principles from the ontological point of view. As the Manichaean heresy is constantly reviving, in an open or secret form, it is important to return to these definitions which the Church has applied to its own thought, continuing the collective work of the Fathers, and especially St Augustine.

MAN'S SUPERNATURAL DESTINY

We have seen how Christian thought in the first centuries, faithful to the principles of biblical anthropology, rejected a certain number of Platonic, Neoplatonic and Gnostic theories, and thus became aware of its own anthropology. Man is created. The human soul is created. It is not part of the divine substance. The soul does not exist before its bodily state. Man is created, soul and body together. From the time of St Justin and St Irenaeus we find Christian thought becoming aware of its inevitable opposition to dualism of the Platonic type. This tendency to unify the human compound finds almost perfect expression, though still sometimes uncertain, in St Thomas Aquinas, who, in principle, adopts the Aristotelian as opposed to the Platonic anthropology, but, in fact, wavers in a number of passages between the two.

But this is not all. The Gnostic myths, like the Neoplatonic philosophy, taught that the human soul is divine by nature. It is a part of the godhead fallen into an evil body. Christian thought rejects this doctrine of a natural consubstantiality of the soul with God, but it presents a doctrine of divinization, which the Greek fathers called *theiosis*.

Man is an animal which is "divinizable". The expression comes from St Gregory Nazianzen. The priestly recital about creation at the beginning of our Bibles teaches that man was created to the image and likeness of God. Scholars have noticed that the theologians who composed this passage set themselves expressly against the Egyptian and Assyro-Babylonian myths, which taught the consubstantiality of the soul with the divinity. Man was not created from God's substance, his spittle, his seed, or his blood; he was created "to the image and likeness" of God. Orthodox Christian thought, rejecting the Gnostic myth which taught the consubstantiality of the soul with God, thus continued in the same line, *in eodem sensu et in eadem sententia*, the thought and purpose of the priestly theology of the fifth century B.C.

What is meant by this doctrine that man is in the image and likeness of God? Many works have been devoted to this subject by the Fathers, but I shall not delay over the subject here. I shall simply mention that with these words the theology of the priestly code opened out a field which is strictly supernatural. Man is not an animal, like other living things. Man is created to the image and likeness of God. Do we not sometimes see on the faces of men and women traces of that strictly supernatural beauty which witnesses to an order not of this world? According to Catholic theology man is called to a strictly supernatural destiny, that is to say, he is called to share in the very nature of God, *consortes divinae naturae*, as we are told in the epistle of St Peter, the words being used in the Missal. The purpose of creation was not merely to bring about a group of spirits living together peacefully before God in a just and happy society. The purpose of creation, the supernatural goal of creation, according to God's plan as it actually is, is a union, a marriage, a fundamental transformation, a divinization, of human nature. The image of marriage is suggested from the time of the Old Testament by the prophets, by Osee, Jeremias and Ezechiel. Union between God and his people is expressed in terms of the marriage analogy; it is the union of lover and beloved spoken of in the Song of Songs, which is the great midrash of the Old Testament, the priceless key to all the Scriptures, opening to us and summing up the mystery of mysteries, the very meaning of creation. In the New Testament the analogy of wedding and marriage is repeated many times. Christ is the bridegroom. At Cana he changes the water of human nature into wine. St Paul teaches in his epistles that the marriage of man and woman is a great secret, a great mystery, for it signifies that blessed union between Christ and his Church. Even the doctrine of the union between the Word of God and human nature can be symbolized by the image of marriage. In the union between the divine nature and human nature, which remain distinct, in the one person of Christ, there is free consent and divinization of human nature, which is the principle of the divinization brought about in mankind by Christ. Christ is thus the germ of the new human race divinized in him and by him, the head of that body, which is the Church, wherein mankind is already really, though partially, supernaturalized and dwelt in by the holy Trinity, sanctified and divinized.

This strictly supernatural destiny of man involves certain metaphysical implications and presuppositions. That man should be able to be called to this godlike destiny, he must be free to consent. Plato writes in the Laws that man is a puppet fashioned by the gods: it is precisely this, a puppet, that man is not, in the eyes of Christianity. God cannot invite a lifeless thing to share in the personal life of the Holy Trinity. Previous conditions are thus necessary, in order that this supernatural destiny may be possible. Man is created for his supernatural destiny. In his very structure a preadaptation to this supernatural destiny should be discernible. Man is an animal which has fourteen thousand millions of neurons in his brain, three times more than the most highly developed monkey. This infinitely complex structure of the human brain renders language possible, and language renders thought possible. Man is an animal capable of understanding the word addressed to him by God. And in order for him to be capable of this a certain biological structure is required, since man is not a pre-existing soul fallen into a body, but a psychological organism, living and spiritual. An animal is also living, and possessed of an animal soul. But what distinguishes man from the animal is precisely that man is capable of a supernatural destiny offered him by grace, and is able to understand the invitation to this spiritual destiny and to correspond with it. It is this capacity which is, I think, meant by the technical term, *spirit*, called by the Old Testament *ruach* and by St Paul *pneuma*.

According to the Old Testament, the beasts are also "living souls". Biblical anthropology is entirely opposed, above all, to Cartesian mechanism and to the idea that animals are machines. The animal is a living thing, that is to say, it possesses an animal soul. But only a man possesses a *spirit*, a *pneuma*, that is, the capacity to receive in himself the *Pneuma* of God, the capacity to lay himself open to the supernatural, the capacity to hear God's word, in short, the capacity for God. This capacity for God, the fact of being able to attain God, is perhaps what best explains in the clearest way the idea of spirit. Biological, empirical, tests are not enough to determine with sufficient ontological precision that which distinguishes man from animal. Neither language, nor conceptual, abstractive intelligence, nor social life, nor capacity to make tools or works of art are tests strict enough to distinguish man from animal. In the animal kingdom, in various degrees and stages, we find traces of an intelligent use of symbols and of abstraction, of language, social life and aesthetic appreciation. From the ontological point of view, from the standpoint of Christian ontology and anthropology, what defines man precisely is the supernatural destiny offered him by grace, for which he is preadapted by creation. What really causes man to be a spirit is that he is capable of attaining God, being called to share in God's life. The philosopher should be able to discover by metaphysical analysis, in concrete human nature as shown us today, traces and signs which reveal that characteristic preadaptation to a supernatural destiny.

The Fathers of the Church saw clearly that freedom was one of the characteristic features involved in man's destiny. Freedom alone can be made like to God, and divinizable by grace. God does not create gods in spite of themselves. The gift of divinization is not received without consent and a new birth freely accepted, brought about by grace, though with the cooperation of human freedom.

Thus the Fathers have all criticized every theory and philosophy in the world which did away with human freedom. A few examples will be enough. Thus Justin writes:

> It is not by the law of destiny that what man does or suffers comes about: everyone does good or evil freely. . . . This is what the Stoics did not understand, for they said that everything obeyed the law of destiny. No, at the beginning God made men and angels their own masters. . . . Every creature is capable of good and evil: there could be no merit, if there were no choice between two courses (*Apology*, 2, 7).

So, too, Tatian:

> Thus the heavenly Logos, spirit born of spirit, reason proceeding from the power of reason, has created man to the likeness of the Father who begot him; he has made of him the image of immortality, in order that, as there is incorruptibility in God, so too man may share in that which is the lot of divinity, and may possess immortality. But, before creating man, the Logos created the angels; and these two orders of creatures have been made free, not possessing by nature the good which is only essential in God, and which in men is realized by their free choice" (*Speech to the Greeks*, 7).

Irenaeus of Lyons, in his great book against heresies, writes: "Man is endowed with reason, and in this he is like to God: he has been created free, left to his own devices, and master of himself" (*Adv. Haer.*, 4, 4, 3). "In the beginning God created man free, so that he should willingly follow God's will, without being forced by God. For God does not use force" (4, 37, 1). If it is by nature that some were made evil and others good, the latter would not be worthy of praise for being good, since they would have been created so, nor would the former be worthy of blame, having also been made so. But in fact all are of the same nature, able to do good and able, on the other hand, to reject it (4, 37, 2). In this passage Irenaeus establishes the very important distinction between nature and freedom, often referred to by the Fathers. Man cannot be good in the sense that a non-living thing is good. His excellence must be a willed excellence, consented to and the fruit of his choice. Thus he could be good in a way like God, who is essentially, but also freely, good. Man, a creature, must cooperate in his own creation.

It is not only, continues St Irenaeus, in his works, but also in his faith that God has left man free and subject to his own choice (4, 37, 5).

It would have been better, say our Gnostic opponents, that God should not have made the angels fallible and capable of sin, and man able to rebel against God. Men and angels have been created with the gifts of reason and free judgement, not, like lifeless things, compelled to do whatever their nature insists on. If the situation were such as our opponents suppose, man's goodness would not be worth gaining, and God's gift of himself would have no value; man would not need to desire the good, which would come to him without any personal wish or trouble or thought on his part: man would receive the goodness, granted him by God, automatically, with no effort, like a lifeless thing. Goodness would be without value, because things would be naturally good, not by choice, because they would be endowed with their goodness automatically, and not by their free will. Moreover, it would follow that they would be incapable of real enjoyment of the beauty of goodness. What enjoyment of goodness can beings have who are without knowledge? (4, 37, 6).

The Gnostics taught that the first man was created with every natural and supernatural gift. The first man, whom the Kabbalistic writings call *Adam Kadmon*, is, moreover, according to the Gnostic systems, not so much created as generated from the divine substance. The first man is a virtue, a power, sent forth by the father God. The Gnostic first man is more like what Christian theology calls the Word of God than what Scripture calls created man. According to the different Gnostic systems, a mythical fall produced, in the divine spheres, a disaster from which came our creation as it is. Gnosticism assigns value to what came first, what is past, what is primitive. Man's salvation, according to Gnosticism, consists in a return to his primitive, previous, original state. The soul was by nature divine; it fell into an evil body, an evil world. Its salvation consists in freeing itself from the bonds of this material and evil world, and in returning to its primitive and original state. Thus the Gnostic myth is cyclic. A happy primitive state, a fall and a return to the primitive state mark its three moments.

With this cyclic conception of destiny Irenaeus contrasts the Christian view of history and creation, which is not cyclic but vectorial. Creation cannot be compared to an original fall which must be put right. Creation is a positive act willed by God. Perfection, completion, what St Paul calls *pleroma*, is ahead of us, in the future. As St Paul writes, forgetting what we have left behind we press on towards the future, like a good athlete, with nothing but the goal in view, when he will receive the prize.

Throughout the centuries and still today, Christians often confuse the Gnostic myth of the fall and the return with the biblical account of sin, or, more accurately, they superimpose the Gnostic idea of the fall upon the Jahvist account in the third chapter of Genesis which deals with man's sin. Now the two doctrines have no connection. It is insufficient to say they have no connection, for they are contradictory.

According to the biblical teaching, creation is a positive act, willed by God and blessed by him. According to Gnosticism, creation is a fall, a disaster. According to the Bible, material creation is willed by God for its own sake. According to Gnosticism, matter is the supreme evil, and God could not have willed material reality. According to the Bible, God created man with a body. According to Gnosticism, the soul pre-existed as part of the divine substance, and it fell into an evil body. According to Gnosticism, creation and the fall are the same. According to Scripture, creation is something quite different from man's sin. According to Gnosticism, creation and the fall are one thing, for which God is responsible. The fall is God's fall. According to the Bible, creation is God's work, and sin is man's work.

According to Gnosticism, creation and the fall constitute a single disaster, to be found at the origin of all things. According to Scripture, man's sin occurs relatively late, and is to be found at the end of creation, for man is the last thing created.

According to Gnosticism, the first man is a mythical being, and the fall is a no less mythical event. According to Scripture, the first man is a historic fact and man's sin is something given in experience. According to Gnosticism, original sin is a precosmic, prehistorical, pre-empirical, fall. According to Scripture, sin is one of the data in our history.

Finally, according to Gnosticism, man, as he exists, is only a degenerate and degraded descendant of the mythical first man. Man as he exists is the result of various disasters, which the Gnostic systems describe in much detail. According to Scripture, man, as he exists, is of the same nature as this first man, or this first mankind, which was created at the beginning.

We see that in every point the Gnostic myth is opposed to the teaching of Scripture.

St Irenaeus, who disputed with the Gnostics, his chief work being called "a refutation of the falsely-called Gnosis or knowledge", attacked the Gnostic myth for this mythical praise of the past, the previous and the primitive, and contrasts with the Gnostic myth the Christian view of things.

Contrary to the teaching of the Gnostic myth, man, explains St Irenaeus, has not been created in a perfect state from the beginning. Undoubtedly God possessed in himself the power to create man in a perfect state from the beginning, for everything is possible to him. But the creation of man involves metaphysical conditions of a special kind. A mother could give a child food fit for a grown-up person, but the child cannot take it. So, too, God is certainly capable of making man perfect from the beginning, but man was unable to take this, for he was like an infant newly born. Irenaeus here makes a profound remark about the metaphysical conditions of man's creation. Once again, man is not a puppet fashioned by the gods, as Plato says. A non-living thing can easily be created complete and perfect, but man is not a thing like this. Man is a being called to share in God's life, a being created to the image and likeness of God. This divine completion, which God wills to give to man, God cannot give in the same way as a colour or any other quality is given or imposed. A man must grow, and must cooperate in his own development, so that he may be truly created in God's image and likeness, and not be a thing created passively. In this passage (*op. cit.*, 4, 38) Irenaeus insists at length and with force on this fact that man was created in an imperfect state, in a state analogous to childhood, and can only gradually receive the good that God wishes to communicate to him. (I have translated all this passage in my book, already referred to, pp. 659 *et seq.*) Irenaeus concludes: "Hence those are thoroughly unreasonable who do not await the time of growth, and blame God for the weakness of their nature." Irenaeus shows how, by an inner and strictly metaphysical necessity, creation is gradual, and, more so, is that divinization which God offers to men. Perfection is not in the past, behind us, but in the future, at the end of God's work, in front of us. The prophets of Israel never turn towards the primitive past of mankind, towards the time which went before man's sin. The prophets and the whole Old Testament have always looked and aimed towards the future, towards the final end, the completion of God's work. Man was not created at the beginning in the full enjoyment of the destiny promised him. As St Irenaeus also writes in the same passage, "We were not able to bear the power of divinity". It is at the end of time that he comes, in whom we receive completion. To the Gnostic myth which assigns highest value to the past and the primitive, Irenaeus oppose the Christian idea of history, which gives highest value to the end, the completion, the *pleroma*.

Many centuries later, in the twentieth century, Fr Teilhard de Chardin, by an objective and scientific analysis of creation as it developed, revived the views expressed by St Irenaeus in the second century, sometimes in the same terms. Against Fr Teilhard's view of history, Gnostic theories, more or less clearly recognized as such, have very often been proposed, which confuse the biblical teaching about man's sin with the Gnostic myth of the fall and the Christian doctrine of redemption with the Gnostic myth of the soul's return to its former state. There are often, too, Gnostic theories which are at work, unnoticed, in political opinions that both idealize in mythical fashion the old order and reject the notion of human progress and a creation really at work in history, as also the idea of biological evolution, and for the same reasons. The idea of evolution and the idea of human or social progress mean that perfection and completion are in front of us, and not behind us in a mythical past. They are things to be done, not to be regretted. They are objects, not for a hopeless nostalgia, but for human effort, cooperating with the creative and saving grace of God.

St Irenaeus laid the first stones of a view of history, Christian and positive and progressive.

Tertullian touched on this problem of the metaphysical implications of man's creation in his book against Marcion. Whence comes evil? asked the Marcionites, and, more generally, all the Gnostic heretics. If God is good and almighty, he should not have allowed man to fall into sin, misery and death. The objection, of course, is an old one and is ever renewed.

Tertullian explains very rightly what is God's plan. Man was created to the image and likeness of God. There is nothing in man which is more to the image and likeness of God than freedom. Man was created free, left to his own choice (*Adversus Marcionem*, 2, 5, 1-2). Man could not be created to the image and likeness of God unless he were created free and independent, able to take up his life as a rational being. God alone is good by nature. Man is good by creation, but he is called to be good through free, personal, consent. Man is called to confirm the perfection offered him, so that this perfection may be not only a natural good—like that of a non-living thing or an animal—but a good which man may deserve (2, 6, 4-5). The creation of man implied that fundamental freedom by which man was rendered capable of confirming the good offered him, but not imposed upon him. The possibility of doing evil is thus implied in the gift of freedom, which is a good. Heretics would like to do away with this fundamental good on account of the consequences, often disastrous, of human freedom. This, however, is to wish to do away with the very work and plan of God for mankind. By creating man free God, so to speak, took on himself the duty to respect man's freedom, and this God has done. That is why God does not intervene forcibly to prevent the designs of human freedom from being carried out. If God intervened, heretics might justly accuse God of fickleness and inconstancy, of infidelity to his own plan (2, 6–7).

The problem of evil cannot be dealt with unless we take into account this plan of God for man: such is the teaching of the Fathers.

After Irenaeus and Tertullian, the Fathers, one and all, claimed for man that freedom which is his dignity and greatness and which makes him a being worthy of God, created to God's image and likeness. Bardesanes of Edessa, in a Syriac dialogue against a dualist heretic in the second century, the Pseudo-Hippolytus, author of the *Elenchos,* then Clement of Alexandria, Origen, Methodius of Olympus, Athanasius of Alexandria, Cyril of Jerusalem, Basil of Caesarea, Gregory of Nyssa, Ambrose, Augustine, and many others, indeed all the Fathers, insist on human freedom, the pledge of a divine calling, and defend it against the astrologers, fatalists, Gnostics and Manichees, the determinists of every kind. (I have quoted a number of passages, *op. cit.,* pp. 668 *et seq.*). It is not matter which is the cause of evil. Evil is the work of created freedom. This created freedom is itself a good. Freedom is "that royal quality which raises man up" above other creatures, as St Gregory of Nyssa tells us (*The Creation of Man,* 4). The greatest of the goods included under "the image and likeness of God" is freedom. Augustine, in his struggle against the Manichees, claims for human freedom responsibility for the evil that man does and criticizes the confusion involved in laying responsibility on a mythical "matter" for the crimes which man commits.

CONCLUSION

At the end of this short essay the reader will doubtless see that there is indeed an original Christian metaphysic, and that the Fathers were aware they possessed a philosophy which in relation to the non-Christian philosophies was original. We have noticed how the Fathers rejected the most characteristic metaphysical theories of Platonism, of Neoplatonism and to some extent even of Aristotelianism: eternity of matter, eternity and divinity of the cosmos, the divine nature of the soul, the cyclic conception of becoming and so on. We have noticed how, when faced with metaphysical theories which they thought incompatible with the inner and essential requirements of Christianity, the Fathers became aware of these metaphysical principles of Christianity and formulated them. Thus Christianity implies an original ontology, based on the distinction between uncreated Being and created being, an original doctrine of the absolute, a doctrine of the relations between the absolute and the world, a cosmology which rejects deification of the universe, and asserts at the same time both its reality and its radical insufficiency to account by itself for its existence, nature and history; an anthropology no less original, which rejects the ancient theories of Orphism and Platonism, and adopts the principles of biblical anthropology. Christian thought, from the patristic age, has been aware of possessing a doctrine of human freedom, of action and of thought, which was to be gradually worked out, through the struggles with the Manichees and the Pelagians, and which was to be affirmed anew from the time of the reaction against the Lutheran theology.

It is difficult, then, to see why a historian like E. Bréhier has been able to deny, in his *Histoire de la Philosophie,* that Christianity involved a strictly philosophical content. Such a denial can only be explained by ignorance of the writings of the Fathers, which are put aside by the historians of philosophy with a contempt tolerated in the teaching of philosophy at the universities. If there is a history of philosophical and metaphysical thought, then the thought of the Fathers forms a part of it, quite as much as that of Plotinus, Porphyry or Proclus, to name only their contemporaries. I have shown that the Fathers *reason.* They are not content to assert the metaphysical ideas contained in Scripture and essential to Christian dogmatic teaching. When they reject Platonic, Neoplatonic or Gnostic theories, they employ reason, they act in the strict sense as philosophers. When, against Plotinus, they assert that the stars are not gods, they cannot be accused of violating the demands of reason and rational scientific method. On the contrary, as Pierre Duhem has emphasized in his masterly and monumental *Système du Monde,* they leave the field open to modern science. Neglect of patristic thought, therefore, lacks any sufficient ground, if we take into account the most exacting rationalism. In my opinion the work of Christian thought in the first centuries has the especial character of a work of reason to get rid of myth. If we see what the Platonists, Neoplatonists and Gnostics of every type taught, this is enough to make us realize that Christian thought, in comparison with the sects around it, appears like a wise and sober person amid others who are drunk with myths and theosophic speculations, with theories which are often fantastic.

It is this character of reason, balance and wisdom which impresses me personally, in the great stream of patristic thought. Faced with systems that depreciate and despise matter, the body, the world and creation, Christian thought teaches the excellence of this creation, and rejects the notions accepted by modern psychopathology: these are notions that trouble the sick. Someday Gnosticism and Manichaeism should be subjected to psycho-analysis. The psychologist and psycho-therapeutist should realize that Christian orthodoxy is found on the side of balance, wisdom and sanity.

Of course the rise of Christian philosophy in the early centuries did not come about without false starts, hesitations and mistakes. But, I may venture to say, the mistakes are still more significant and important than the steady development of biblical thought and orthodox Christian thought. For the mistakes, for instance, of Origen, or of Gregory of Nyssa (concerning sex), allow Christian thought as a whole to react, to examine itself, to express itself often with vigour and then to define its own beliefs. Thus the Origenist crisis was important for the growth of Christian philosophy. We see how Christian thought as a whole reacted against the theories of one of its most subtle teachers, against one of the most brilliant intellects of a great century. Christian thought is independent of even the greatest genius. It did not adopt all the teaching of Irenaeus, Tertullian, Origen, Gregory of Nyssa, Jerome or Augustine. Christian thought chooses freely and authoritatively what is suitable to it. What is not suitable it rejects or allows to be forgotten. To forget things is a sign of health. It does not seem profitable or wise to wish to popularize all the teachings of the Fathers for their own sakes. Some are out of date, useless at the present day, and the oblivion into which they have fallen is their best fate. But it is through the Fathers that Christian thought has been formed, and for this reason the Fathers remain indispensable as witnesses to it. They have caused the thought of the Church to grow; their works live after them, we may say, for ever, in the souls they have helped to perfect.

The period which we have been considering is only the first, the period of youth, in Christian thought. It is the period during which the main lines of Christian thought became established. In this respect it is a privileged period, just as to the biologist the embryonic period is privileged, when growth is most intense, and the differentiation of tissues and cells most significant. Broadly speaking, both from the metaphysical and from the theological point of view the structure of Christian thought had already become established by the time of St Augustine's death. It is of utmost interest to read again today the great works of this time when Christian thought was formed, for it was a period of creative life, unique of its kind.

After St Augustine a period of hidden life seemed to follow. In the twelfth century, and then still more in the thirteenth, a fresh crisis of growth allowed Christian metaphysics to become aware once again of what had already been accepted, and to become aware, in new respects, of its own principles, its own metaphysical needs. In the twelfth century, against the Neo-Manichaean dualists, in the thirteenth century when faced with the movement of Neoplatonizing Aristotelianism, Christian thought lived through a crisis of growth as acute as that of the first centuries. Christian thought returned to the problems we have considered here: eternity or non-eternity of the world and of matter, the problem of the soul, the problem of evil, the problem of time against those who, like Siger de Brabant, reintroduced the myth of the everlasting return, the problem of individuation against those who, following in the steps of Neoplatonism, held that matter alone could cause individuation, a theory which rendered the ontological position of the human person unintelligible. But from the thirteenth century, Christian thought opened out fresh problems, in particular that of knowledge. Christian thought became aware of the implications of its principles in regard to epistemology. That, however, is another story, to which perhaps one day I shall return.

After the great crisis of the thirteenth century, once again there was, it seems, a period of hidden life, especially in the eighteenth and nineteenth centuries. Nevertheless Christian thought never ceased to be aware of itself, and of its inner, essential, demands. It continued to grow in wisdom and in age. Nor is the work of Christian philosophy finished. Faced with non-Christian or anti-Christian philosophies, such as those of Fichte, Schelling, Hegel, Marx or Nietzsche, Christian thought needs workmen who, like St Irenaeus when faced with the Gnostics, or Augustine when faced with the Manichees, can detect the falsehood of a pretended wisdom, unmask the ancient myths embedded in metaphysical systems that claim to be scientific, practise discernment of spirits.

In the twentieth century there seem signs of a renaissance. The authors of the Thomist revival, Christian philosophers like Blondel and Laberthonnière, have been setting themselves once again to reflect on the metaphysical principles at the basis of Christianity, feeling their way, as always happens with human enterprises, amid struggles which are inevitable and not always without their fruit. The return to Scripture will probably make it possible to get a clearer appreciation of the metaphysical principles of Christianity, already contained, explicitly or implicitly, in the two Testaments. For, it will be noticed, Christian thought, in the first centuries and later, has remained true to the revealed deposit, in the metaphysical as well as in the theological sphere. In spite of appearances, in spite of successive restatements, Christian thought is like the growth of a tree, as it carries on biblical thought. Spiritually we are Hebrews, children of Abraham.

SELECT BIBLIOGRAPHY

In this series: BRUNOT, Amédée, S.C.J.: *St Paul and his Message*; CRISTIANI, Léon: *Heresies and Heretics*; CAYRÉ, F., A.A.: *The First Spiritual Writers*; NÉDONCELLE, M.: *Is there a Christian Philosophy?*

ALTANER, B.: *Patrology*, London and New York, Nelson, 1960.

BARDY, G.: *The Church at the End of the First Century*, London, Sands, 1938.

CARROLL, Paul (Editor): *Letters of St Jerome*, Chicago, Regnery, 1954.

CAYRÉ, F.: *A Manual of Patrology and the History of Theology*, Paris, Desclée, 1956.

COLEBURT, R.: *An Introduction to Western Philosophy*, New York, 1957, and London, 1958, Sheed and Ward.

COPLESTON, F., S.J.: *A History of Philosophy*, six volumes (to date), London, Burns and Oates, and Westminster, Md, Newman Press, 1946—.

D'ARCY, M., S.J., and others: *A Monument to St Augustine*, London and New York, Sheed and Ward, 1930.

DE LUBAC, H., S.J.: *Catholicism*, translated by Lancelot C. Sheppard, London, Burns and Oates, and New York, Longmans, 1950.

LEBRETON, J., and ZEILLER, J.: *The History of the Primitive Church*, translated by Ernest C. Messenger, four volumes, London, Burns and Oates, 1942–8, and New York, Macmillan.

MARROU, H. I.: *History of Education in Antiquity*, translated by G. Lamb, London and New York, Sheed and Ward, 1956.

OATES, Whitney J.: *Basic Writings of St Augustine*, two volumes, New York, Random House, 1948.

OULTON, J., and CHADWICK, H. (Editors): *Alexandrian Christianity*, London, S.C.M., and Philadelphia, Westminster Press, 1954.

POURRAT, P.: *Christian Spirituality*, Volume I, London, Burns and Oates, 1922, and Westminster, Md, Newman Press, 1953.

PRESTIGE, G. L.: *God in Patristic Thought*, London, Macmillan, 1952.

PRZYWARA, E.: *An Augustine Synthesis*, London and New York, Sheed and Ward, 1951.

QUASTEN, J.: *Patrology,* two volumes, Westminster, Md, Newman Press, 1950 and 1953.

QUASTEN, J., and PLUMPE, J. C. (Editors): *Ancient Christian Writers:* the Works of the Fathers in translation. A series of translations into English of which to date some thirty-four volumes have appeared. Westminster, Md, Newman Press, and London, Longmans, 1946—.

RAND, E. K.: *Founders of the Middle Ages,* Cambridge, Mass., Harvard Univ. Press, 1928.

The Twentieth Century Encyclopedia of Catholicism

The number of each volume indicates its place in the over-all series and not the order of publication.

TWENTIETH CENTURY ENCYCLOPEDIA OF CATHOLICISM

All titles are subject to change.